William P. Talboys

West India pickles

Diary of a cruise through the West Indies in the yacht Josephine

William P. Talboys

West India pickles
Diary of a cruise through the West Indies in the yacht Josephine

ISBN/EAN: 9783744756495

Printed in Europe, USA, Canada, Australia, Japan

Cover: Foto ©Andreas Hilbeck / pixelio.de

More available books at **www.hansebooks.com**

IN PREPARATION.

—

FLORIDA ORANGES.

BY

W. P. TALBOYS,

AUTHOR OF

"West India Pickles."

DIARY OF A CRUISE THROUGH THE WEST INDIES

IN THE YACHT JOSEPHINE.

[New York Yacht Club.]

By W. P. TALBOYS.

WITH NUMEROUS ILLUSTRATIONS.

NEW YORK:

G. W. Carleton & Co., Publishers.

LONDON: S. LOW, SON & CO.

MDCCCLXXVI.

To

M. E. W. S.,

ONE OF MY EARLIEST FRIENDS IN AMERICA,

THESE PAGES ARE

AFFECTIONATELY INSCRIBED.

" We left behind the painted buoy
    That tosses at the harbor-mouth ;
And madly danced our hearts with joy,
    As fast we fleeted to the South :
How fresh was every sight and sound
    On open main or winding shore !
We knew the merry world was round,
    And we might sail for evermore.

By peaks that flamed, or, all in shade,
    Gloom'd the low coast and quivering brine
With ashy rains, that spreading made
    Fantastic plume or sable pine ;
By sands and steaming flats, and floods
    Of mighty mouth, we scudded fast,
And hills and scarlet-mingled woods
    Glow'd for a moment as we past.

O hundred shores of happy climes,
    How swiftly stream'd ye by the bark !
At times the whole sea burned, at times
    With wakes of fire we tore the dark ;
At times a carven craft would shoot
    From havens hid in fairy bowers,
With naked limbs and flowers and fruit,
    But we nor paused for fruit nor flowers."

TENNYSON.

CONTENTS.

PREFACE.

THE following pages pretend to no literary merit. They are merely the transcript of a daily jotting down of the scenes and occurrences of our cruise, and were intended, not for publication, but to serve as an aid to those pleasures of memory which are truly the very best part of a traveller's enjoyment.

My friend, Mr. Carleton, having waded through the original smudgy pencilled notes, in an unguarded moment expressed a desire to publish them, and I only hope he will not regret his generous imprudence.

We sailed from the harbor of New York in the first days of November, and having determined to visit as many of the West India Islands as possible, our stay in each place was necessarily very short:—my notes, therefore, have no geographical or scientific statistics—indeed I rather hope that the gentle reader will favorably appreciate my abstinence in this respect.

I ask indulgence for the details and descriptions of the sailing and yachting part of the journal, which I have retained in the hope that they will convey some information to yachtsmen who may visit those waters; and also because I desire to record faithfully the admirable sea-going qualities and behavior of the "Josephine." Although a centre-board schooner, she draws 8 ft. 2 in., and hence her great steadiness in heavy sea-ways, as her board was practically little used, except in smooth water. Her tonnage (in old measurement) is 143 tons, and her length 95½ feet over all. She carried a crew of two mates and four seamen, exclusive of the cook, mate, and steward, but was entirely commanded and navigated by her owner, and by his admirable seamanship our comfort and enjoyment were well secured.

A journal, after all, is but a scrap of autobiography, and like Charles I., in Mr. Dick's Kite, the objectionable pronoun "I" *will* get in, so I make no apology in this respect—all I can say is,

"Vive, vale—si quid novisti rectiûs istis,"
"Candidus imperti : si non, his utere mecum."

UNION CLUB, *August*, 1875.

INTRODUCTION.

IT was last summer, while gently heaving on the long blue swell, along the
pleasant shores of Massachusetts, and off the
lovely harbor of Beverley, we were cruising
about in the little "Josephine," whose portrait
adorns the frontispiece. Far from the madding
crowd, it was bliss just to breathe the soft
Atlantic air, and lazily watch the fleet of fishing schooners pursuing the mackerel. Not
a word had been spoken for an hour, when
suddenly our skipper, dear old L——, beloved
of gods and men (also of women), waking from
a long dream of peace, broke the silence with:
"Will you go with me to the West Indies in
her, for a cruise, next winter?" To which I
responded: "Won't I? Like a bird!"

This was, perhaps, a hasty decision; but
what clever creature was it who said: "Always

act on your first impulses, for they *may* be good!" And, indeed, who could stop to consider duties or weigh possibilities, even with the *duris urgens in rebus egestas* forever gnawing at his heart, when such a glorious prospect was suddenly unfolded; for this was not to be a mere trip to the Cockney tropics, such as Nassau or Havana have become, but a long cruise through the Windward Islands, a certain Odyssean coasting of cape, promontory, rock and hill; dropping the anchor in places of which the names alone stirred in one vague, spicy ideas of nodding palms, luscious fruits, perpetual verdure, golden weather, "gems and gem-like eyes"—all the languid, passionate fancies that hang round the Tropics, and have a wild fascination for those who know them only by hearsay.

But it was not until the tall golden rods had burned themselves to death on Beverley's parched hill-sides, and every autumn-tinted leaf was fluttering down, that on one auspicious hazy afternoon L—— told us to be ready to sail the following morning. And I was ready—yet, with every pulse beating with the prospect of enjoyment, I felt, as Emerson so cleverly points out, that compensations lie on both sides of happiness, and it was not without a wrench that I said good-by to the kid who stood waving his farewells with a big complimentary tear in each blue eye. As I stepped into the cab that was to take me to the wharf, I recognized that no man who leaves home, whether for pleasure or in the pursuit of profit, can sever, even for a few months, all the silken fetters of his life without feeling that he must " drag at each remove a lengthening chain."

The chain, however, seemed light and wrapped in velvet when I first caught sight of the pretty schooner, riding at anchor, bright with fresh paint—her white decks glittering in the morning sun, her foretopmast sent ashore, and the mainsail reduced from the great racing canvas of the summer cruise, to fitting proportions, gently flapping in the light Indian-summer breeze. A moment's bustle, a word or two here and there, with the friends who had come to bid us God-speed, and we were in tow of a tug. Opposite Fort Columbus—where our other sails being hoisted, we clasped hands and parted with a cheer—one dear fellow, as he stepped over the side to the tug's deck, cried out, "Tal, keep a journal!" I have done so —and here it is.

THE JOURNAL.

November 7th, 1874.—Not long after the tug
left us, just half drifting down the Bay, we mustered in the cabin for our first repast, L—— having ordered lunch as quickly as possible, on the
principle, I fancy, that in England they always
butter a cat's paws on bringing it to a strange
house: at any rate, emotions of the mind are
very favorable to the appetite. We mustered
five: L—— (the captain), C—— and myself,
who had shipped for the whole cruise, and H——
and W——, who had joined us for the run to St.
Thomas. The discussion of our destination and a
little gentle scandal wore off the novelty of our
situation, and the breeze freshened a little; but
before we reached Sandy Hook, C—— went to

sleep—alas, he snored !—and the wind instantly changed and came out ahead.

November 8th.—Wind ahead all night, smooth sea, and gorgeous morning. I was wakened at dawn by the earliest pipe of half-awakened birds in the shape of a horrid row made by the live ducks on deck—wretched creatures, upon whom a future liver complaint is beginning to dawn. The wind remained ahead, C—— having adhered to his practices through the night ; but at 2 P.M., off Barnegat Light

> " We looked our last on *sand* and plain,
>   As what we ne'er might see again,"

L—— having tacked ship, and with a fine whole sail breeze we head S.E. bound for St. Thomas, turning our backs upon the long reach of sand glittering in the sun, which I am told is Barnegat. Everything hitherto has been delightful, except that, early this morning, the demon *mal-de-mer* boarded us, and the young and imaginative Harry became his first victim. Nobly he bears up, but his eye is fishy, and very sickly his smile ; reclining on deck, he steadily refused cocktails and all consolation, until, in despair, he has turned in. *Requiescat in pace.*

Inconsolable.

In the afternoon, the fine breeze and approaching dinner cheer everybody, and the day ends very pleasantly. I observe, however, that C—— plays bézique far too well for private life.

Monday, November 9th.—The sun shines into the cabin this morning, alike upon the just and the unjust, in the loveliest way, and the very decided change in the temperature shows the progress we have made during the night. Yesterday Ulsters were pleasant on deck; this morning tubs are in season. Just at noon, a little cross-bill bird flew aboard, perched on our heads, enjoyed a slight repast, took a short nap, and after most intimate conduct flew away to leeward.

It was quite a superstitious event, and indeed within an hour or two we got into the Gulf Stream, with a smart W.S.W. breeze; double reefed foresail and mainsail, with maintopmast and flying jibboom both housed; and I venture to say that no yachtsman can ever know to what extent a schooner can roll, pitch, jump, dive and generally waltz about, until he has tried the Gulf Stream under the same circumstances.

Dinner is perhaps, on board a yacht, the most pleasing event in the day's natural sequence, but to-day heavy rain-squalls and the beam-endiness of the lively "Josephine" make us take but a languid interest in that repast, although her behavior in a very trying sea is gratifying. L—— reads aloud from Maury's "Theory of Storms" that we must expect heavy gales about every six days above N. latitude 30°. With such cheerful tales do we beguile the way! As I turn in I imagine, from the sounds that issue from C——'s berth, that we shall have a change of wind.

November 10.—We had a baddish night, but the wind has changed to a moderate N.E. breeze, and joy cometh with the morning. The sea is still very heavy ; " all up in haycocks," the mate calls it, and the water is of the wonderful blue china color peculiar to the Gulf Stream, and great fields of floating Sargasso weed lie all round us. The sun breaks through and touches everything, including our spirits, with his magical wand. The heat becomes really oppressive, and like the traveller in the fable of the Wind and the Sun, we recognize the power of the latter. C——, down in the cabin, has already begun to read about creoles and dark Southern beauties ! As I descend the companion-way he asks me what I should call " expressive feet and ankles ? " He says he is only reading travels, but this is a bad sign.

In the afternoon we pass out of the eastern limit of the Gulf Stream into smoother water, although the masses of floating weed still show themselves. About midnight, after making eight knots for hours under full sail, with a smooth sea, the breeze freshens, and we roll and pitch about in a heavy cross sea under forestaysail, double reefed foresail and maintrysail.

" *Desinit in piscem mulier formosa superne*" · -which means that a fine day ends very fishily

November 11*th.*—The head sea continues, but the wind is nearer abeam, and the weather is exquisite. Of course the decks are wet, and the rolling and jumping goes on as the wind blows half a gale, but we are under light canvas, and the gentle Josephine behaves like a cork with brains. We all show a certain devotion to our repasts, but at other times a gentle languor pervades, and berths are silently sought. One of the privileges of yachting is undoubtedly the pleasure of remaining silent in each other's company without discomfort, and days like these glide by almost without incident, but with a great deal of repose.

November 12*th.*—The sea has been subsiding all night, and we have made good way under easy sail. I came on deck to see a most magnificent sunrise. Our second mate, who is a typical Yankee, clever, confident, most colloquial, and the possessor of strangely amorphous legs, nodded his head towards the resplendent horizon, observing that it was " mighty pooty," which obliged me to admit that it was a neat thing in sunrises.

I was amused too, on walking down into the
cabin again, to observe all three of my fellow-
pilgrims lying asleep—each in his berth, also
on his back, and each with his nose in the air
at a different angle. This adds an expression
of innocence to "the rapture of repose that's
there" that may not be all undeserved. "*Ma-
lus pastor dormit supinus*" is all stuff. The
afternoon finds us with light baffling winds
and calms, a smooth sea, and exquisite weather,
in the calm belt of Cancer.

November 13th.—A smooth sea, wind ahead,
but light and refreshing. The morning is gorgeous, and it is pleasant to be moving along,
although we are four points off our course.
Decks are dry and available for exercise. The
wretched wave-worn ducks and hens in their
coop, forward, salute the sun with faint cack-
lings and quackings, as they absorb their ma-
tutinal corn, shedding a fragrance impossible
to describe, and almost impossible to bear. At
12:30 P. M. we spoke the first vessel we have
seen since leaving Sandy Hook, the barque
"Volunteer," bound for New York. She was

lumbering along before the wind at a speed of about three knots an hour and it really was quite piratical, the saucy way in which our little schooner danced down to her, ran across her bows, tacked, and bore up under her stern, and L—— hailed her with a request to report us. At any rate, it was an event to break the monotony of such summer sailing; and it is a monotony, and beats lotos eating. While we hope, looking over the blue expanse,

" This mounting wave will roll us shoreward soon,"

the languid air swoons all around us, and it would appear to be always afternoon to us, only that it seems always just before dinner, as John (the steward) perpetually seems to be laying the cloth for some repast or other. Now let the merciful trade-winds breathe gently in our favor, and we shall soon hope

" To watch the crisping ripples on the beach,
    And tender curving lines of creamy spray."

November 14*th.*—" *Les jours se suivent et ne se ressemblent pas.*" Yesterday was a long, hot, languid day of calms or light baffling winds; but shortly after midnight, rain-squalls

and alarums ushered us into the trade-winds,
and after running before the fresh north-east
breeze for hours, with all sail set, and making
twelve knots, about noon down came our kites,
and we took two reefs in the mainsail. This
is the first day, since leaving Sandy Hook, that
we have really a fair wind, and now we have
got one with a vengeance. The sun has devour-
ed the clouds that have hid his face all the
morning, and he is giving wonderful trans-
lucent effects to the crests of the great waves
that are chasing us.

8 P.M.—The great waves have increased to
hissing monsters that wish to devour us. We
are in the tail of a north-east gale, and are tearing along before a succession of squalls, under
staysail, close reefed foresail, and reefed maintrysail—the mainsail furled and secured amid-
ships. The handy little boat avails herself of
the opportunity to show her admirable qualities,
skipping in the easiest manner up and down
the watery mountains. As we sat round the
cabin table after dinner, a more than usually
malignant sea broke through the skylight and
deluged us, and we scattered in the most absurd

and rapid manner to the various lounges. With that total depravity which distinguishes inanimate things, the water at once sought and filled the chart-drawer which stood invitingly open, and reduced those valuable articles to a pulpy condition.

There is a general tacit determination among us to take Mr. Greeley's advice, and move West —if we ever get back.

November 15*th.* — The N.E. gale blows stronger than ever, and we really feel a little swindled. We had longed for the trade-winds, having read that as soon as we reached their latitudes a gentle, equal breeze would waft us to our destination, under pleasant skies, with smooth seas and flying fish playing about; and here we are, pitching about in the heaviest sea I ever saw—washed fore and aft all the time, with occasional visitations through the skylight. At night it seems rougher still, and it is a great pleasure to see daylight again. A large flying fish mistook his way and flew on board. He was instantly cooked.

November 16*th.*—Heavy seas and hard squalls

all night. Every wash that broke into the cabin would cause four anxious faces to protrude from four uneasy berths. At dawn the sun rose in almost a clear sky and the strength of a genuine old-fashioned gale. After the noon observations, we found that we were considerably to leeward of the Virgin Pass, and 198 miles from the Mona Pass; and in view of the gale, and the necessity of heaving to and riding it out before we could lay our course for St. Thomas, L—— proposed to run to the southward for Mona Pass, so as to get under the lee of Porto Rico. This will ease the schooner, and the decision is hailed with general applause. It is acted upon at once, a reef turned out of the foresail and trysail, and we bowl along merrily and much more comfortably in our new course S. by E.; still the great white-maned sea-horses rush up astern, and menace us from a great height.

Occasionally the wash from the crest of a wave wets somebody's shirt, but the sun shines out so cheerily over all, his brightness seems to dispel half the discomforts, and to moderate the natural anxieties of a landsman. It

doesn't seem as if anything could happen
with such a bright sunlight, and such a
delicious, soft, warm air. I can't help fancying
that the sailors, who in turn take their trick at
the wheel, have an amused expression, as who
should say, " *I* get $35 a month for slipping
about and getting wet through—but where can
your fun be?" And Andrew, observing a sea
come over her quarter and souse me, remarked
with quite a sardonic grin: " I hope you be a
enjoying of yourself, sir!" But he could not
shake my faith that I was having a good time.
By midnight the gale has moderated to a good
breeze, the sea is smoother, the moon is up, and
we are looking forward to the welcome sound
of " Land, ho!" to-morrow morning.

November 17*th*.—The night has been smooth
and agreeable, and the sun rises very warm,
with a moderate breeze. The winter is past
and gone, the time of the singing birds is
come, and the voice of the turtle ought to be
heard, as we have seen several. At 10 A.M.
we welcome the cry, " Land, ho!" dead ahead,
thirty miles away. It rises in high misty hills,

like a great cloud on the horizon, and is the beautiful island of Porto Rico. We set the mainsail with two reefs, and our valued friend the trysail disappears.

We recognize fully to-day that we are in the tropics. The thermometer stands at 84° in the companion-way, and 95° on deck, and the flying fish skip round us in a lively manner. As we run full before the wind, with all sail made, the sun beats down on our heads as it never seems to at home, even in the dog days, and the cabin is a grateful retreat, especially as it is the home of lemonade and other refreshments. From one great purple roller to another we rapidly approach the island, but unfortunately a bank of heavy clouds rests upon the mountain ranges, and partially veils the great El Yunque (the anvil), the highest peak of the Sierra Luquillo, 3,750 feet high. He is forty miles away, but we can make out the broad square outline from which he is named. After rounding the north-western point of the island, we enter Mona Pass, which is the strait dividing Porto Rico from San Domingo. It is sixty miles broad, and the water, instead of the unvarying blue, softens to the most exquisite silvery green color. At 3 P.M. we run into a little bay on the west coast called Aguadilla, and anchor near two or three other small vessels, opposite a very pretty little village of that name. The village is built close to the water, with a background of beautifully wooded cliffs, and reminds one of Torquay. The church is an edifice of some pretension, but dwarfed in its towers, on account of hurricanes and earthquakes. There is also a fort, mounting two or three aged guns, and a colored sentinel, but no landing-place to be seen, and we observe the natives landing through the surf in large dorys. We had hardly dropped our anchor, when a boat, with an immense Spanish flag and a very small man in the stern, came alongside with such a rush as to call for an expostulation. " *Cuidado you negronis ne scratchez pas the painto?* " was the phrase which appealed to their consideration. The small one was the collector of the port, and finding we had no bill of health from New York, he refused us permission to land, and placed us under quarantine. for twenty-four hours.

Our conversation was poor work, as the sample of Spanish quoted above is about as good as we could muster, and, of course, the small Don was above knowing our heretical language; but as far as one could judge, he was severely troubled in his mind because we had no cargo and, above all, no "*manifiesto*."

The little man left us with the gravest doubts of our respectability, which were heightened by a pretense he made of reading L——'s commission from the Treasury Department, and of which of course he didn't understand one word. He carried this ashore with him, also a letter from us to the U. S. Consular Agent, of an appealing nature. But all the blazing afternoon we swung disregarded, tabooed, and grumbling awfully, although a quiet night will be a good thing for ourselves and the crew.

November 18*th.*—We get a letter from the Consular Agent, telling us in substance what the collector has just told us, as he ran alongside in his nigger manned boat—that our quarantine will be up at 1 P. M. and then we can

1*

go ashore, which we are all longing to do. We
are out of cigars, and the skipper of a Yankee
schooner anchored near us, as he passed under
our stern in his boat, tried to throw one on board
as a sample of what they had ashore; but miss-
ing us it fell in the water. W. K——, who is
a splendid swimmer threw off his clothes, took a
" header " off the taffrail and secured it. We
were immediately hailed from the Yankee
schooner, " I guess you'd better get your man
back, this here bay is full of ground shirks!"
I need not say how delighted we were when he
got safe aboard. I quite sickened with the ex-
pectation of a catastrophe. At half-past one
o'clock two or three or three officers, with a rather uncertain interpreter (for whose services, by-
the-bye, they charged $8.) came off to us, and
after searching and examining the boat, gracious-
ly raised the " taboo," but politely informed us
that we must remain under the guns (!) of the
fort until they could receive instructions from
the Captain General of the island, to whom
they had telegraphed at St. Juan, the capital.
The wise men of Aguadilla seem to be in a
dreadful way about us; they cannot be per-

suaded that anybody would **go** yachting **for** pleasure, and besides the ingenious collector has an **idea** of collecting a fine of $400 from us, for not having the indispensible " *manifesto.*" They have also received intelligence that, " a chiel's among us taking notes," in the shape of **a** reporter for the " N. Y. Herald," who is making drawings, etc. for some dangerous purpose, and to crown all, another schooner flying the **U. S.** flag has just run in, having mistaken the harbor for that of Maynaguez whither she is bound. This scares them terribly, and they have gone ashore to review the troops, and strengthen the **defences.** It is quite evident that the " Virginius " matter is not forgotten.

At last we prepared to land, **but** this is an undertaking. We have observed the landing of several passengers from a coasting steamer that **ran in an hour ago, and,** with all **their** care, **a boatman succeeded** in upsetting one of the **dories, and turning a stout old Don and** his Lares into **the surf, to the** great **delight of a** crowd **of colored** nudities **on the beach.**

At last we reached the shore, **and proceeded with a** long following **of curious niggers, to** visit

Mr. Koppisch, the consular agent for everywhere, who entertained us very pleasantly, and presented us to his charming family. Having been educated in New York, they at least understood the object of a yacht, and by exhibiting our letters the consul was able to soothe in some degree, the alarms of the authorities. We visited the quaint little town and entered the queerly decorated church, without disturbing the devout worshippers, kneeling here and there before the tawdry colored images and pictures.

Church at Aguadilla.

In the centre of the open space in front of the church, stands a time worn sundial still faithfully marking the creeping hours. It had a ruined, forlorn look, as if tired of preaching the terrible legend.

"**Vulnerant** omnes, ultima **necat!**"

They all wound—the last kills!—it is the sentiment of a Trappist.

The question of slavery on this island is definitely set at rest; the slaves have been liberated by a sliding scale of age, and only seven or eight individuals remain in a state of servitude. The free colored population is very large, of different shades of mulatto, and it is amusing to see how the arrogant gravity of the Spaniard is grafted on the indolence of the African. They lounge about with strange expressionless faces, like the musicians in Gerome's picture of the Almée. The sea has been smooth all day, so that we returned on board without any difficulty, and even brought some ladies off in the brilliant moonlight to see the yacht.

November 19*th.*—At dawn, a dug-out came alongside rowed by the dirtiest of darkies, who had a quantity of small red mullets for sale. For twenty-five cents we secured about twenty of them; and the rosy beauties flipped about

the deck until they met their fate in the pan;
and they proved to be perfectly delicious.   We
went ashore to see the market-place, which was
filled with gabbling, chattering negresses selling
fruit, fish, eggs and corn, but there were no
vegetables at all.   We took the opportunity to
lay in a supply of delicious oranges and lemons,
(about five cents a dozen).   I have not seen one
even good-looking woman in the place.   On returning on board we got under way, but drifted
about the bay for some hours, victims of a dead
calm interspersed with rain storms, and every
rain drop is a "douche," as if a string had to be
pulled to produce each one.   The day was disagreeable till sundown; we attempted fishing
and had several bites.   II. R—— landed an odd,
eruptive-looking snapper, white with red spots
all over him, but the breeze springing up, we
hauled in our lines and headed down the Mona
Pass bound to Santa Cruz, 140 miles of dead
beating to windward.

November 20th.--We have fairly entered the
Carribean sea, and enjoy the exquisitely clear,
light blue waters, so different from the heavy

tumbling waves of the Atlantic, on the north coast of the island, and which were characterized most appropriately by a schooner captain, at Aguadilla, as " perfectly *scandalous*." As we glide along several miles from shore, in twelve fathom water, the sand and coral bottom gives the surface a wonderful sheen, as if we were sailing over satin; but we are too far from the land to see any of its beauties, except the lofty outlines of the mountains.

November 21*st*. —Another glorious day!

> " Like the waves of the summer, as one dies away,
> Another as bright and as shining comes on."

We have made about sixty miles along the southern shore, and about five miles from it. The land and sea together have a fanciful resemblance to Mediterranean scenes, and a remarkably good imitation of the Cornici road, so that one can almost see Monaco, or Ventimiglia as we smoothly glide along. A cloudless sky! smooth sea! good breeze! exquisite landscapes! pleasant companions! a certainty of superior repasts in their due seasons! and the hope of a letter from one's true love at St.

Thomas what is wanting to the perfection of yachting, or even the sum of human happiness?

In the afternoon, after standing close in shore on the port tack, we at last take leave of the beautiful, picturesque shores of Porto Rico, and of the mountains overhanging them, where

" Like clouds suspended in an emerald sky,
The ash and the acacia floating hang
Tremulous and pale.   Like restless serpents, clothed
In rainbow and in fire, the parasites
Starr'd with ten thousand blossoms, flow around
The gray trunks.
                    Soft mossy lawns
Beneath these canopies extend their swells,
Fragrant with perfumed herbs, and eyed with blooms
Minute yet beautiful."

A most brilliant moonlight finds us flying along eight knots an hour, and laying our course for the island of Santa Cruz, which already looms on the horizon.

November 22*d*.—I came on deck at daylight to find that we are hove-to off Christianstedt, the small capital of the small island, and waiting for a pilot who is beating out to us through an opening in the coral reef which extends along the whole shore. As we approach the island from the sea, its soft undulat-

ing lines of cane-fields coming close down to
the shore, and the avenues and clusters of cocoa and palms, surrounding the emerald green
with a darker fringe, are all bathed in the glory
of the rising sun, as well as the back-ground of
wooded hills, which in the half-light looked
like a number of coal heaps, but now glitter
out, dotted with sugar plantations and residences. These hills are a little like those we
saw in Porto Rico, but neither so grand, or so
beautiful, the highest being only about a thousand feet high. The island itself though very
small, (only about eighteen miles long, and six
in breadth) seems only cultivated in the western
and northern parts; the eastern end still looks
as wild and as waste as when Columbus first
anchored here in 1493, and appears to be given
over to deer and wild jackasses, which form the
" game" of the island. Christianstedt itself
has a very picturesque appearance, rising in an
amphitheatre from the shore; but while we are
observing these things, the pilot has anchored
us very cleverly close into a stone quay, which
is packed with colored faces, gaping at the
yacht, and jabbering fearfully. We are rid

ing in smooth water, the color of malachite, while beyond us the breakers we have passed through, are booming away upon the coral reef. We at once receive a visit from the Danish officials, who are as polite and amiable as the Aguadilla fellows were unpleasant.

On landing, we were delighted to find a very handsome little town, regularly laid out in squares, clean, well built, and inhabited by an English speaking people of various shades of color, which latter, however, is not surprising, when we remember that there are only 4,000 whites in the whole population of the island, which is 24,000. Our first object ashore was to present letters of introduction to Mr. M——, who is the chief planter and merchant of Santa Cruz; but we were rather dismayed, with the mercury at 90°, on finding that he lived at Fredrichstadt, 15 miles off at the west end, where most of his plantations lie: however, after waiting a tropical length of time, we succeeded in procuring a carriage and a light wagon, in which we had a most delightful excursion through the country, over splendid, hard, smooth, level roads, broad avenues bordered by cocoa

palms, and rolling away through mile after
mile of rich waving fields of sugar cane. Here
and there we met with groups of colored youths
offering, for the absurdly small sum of ten cents,

The Cocoa Palm.

a basket full of green cocoa nuts with which
we quenched our thirst. The results of a too
copious draft suggested the value of a sketch of
brandy in the milk *experto crede !*

At every turn we came to a handsome residence, each with its windmill, sugar houses and laborer's huts all built of stone,—from one end of our ride to the other were evidences of the most industrious cultivation, while the fallow lands were one carpet of exquisite flowers: Euphorbiæ, convolvuli, and the lovely scarlet hibiscus. Everybody we met, whether walking or riding, saluted us in the must polite manner, and this happens also when we walk in the town.

When we arrived at the residence of our friend, it seemed as if all the traditions of planter's hospitality were verified and exalted, so charming was our reception by Mr. M——and his family. It certainly was delightful to sit in a cool veranda, with a splendid view of the ocean, and enjoy a regular gossip about home, with the lovely chatelaine, who also came from New York. It was delightful to mount horses, and scamper off through the woods and over the hills for eight or ten miles, with distant glimpses of the sea at the ends of long ravines of densest verdure, while the hills are carefully cultivated from the very summits. Indeed Mr.

M—— told me that the smooth, rounded appearance of these summits was owing to the fact that the tops *had been cultivated off*—this sounds like the tale of a traveller. We found our host's horses small but easy paced and very sure-footed in trying places. After dinner, resisting with difficulty the kindly invitations of our host, we drove back through the cool dark, with occasional drenching rains, to Christianstedt and the small "Josephine." I took the opportunity of testing the effects of genuine Santa Cruz rum, made on the plantation,—— it is very agreeable, but perhaps insidious.

November 23*d.*—C—— and I—— landed in the cool of the morning, and took a walk about the town. Colored women of every size, shape, hue and feature imaginable, blackest ebony, orange tawney, or café-au-lait, walked about the streets, or hung from the queer wooden balconies that extend from house to house. Some of them were ridiculous resemblances of friends at home, we certainly saw uncle D—— and Mdme. ——. The pretty little Protestant church near the middle of the town possesses an ideal cemetery. How delightful to know that when one has "shuffled off this mortal coil"

A Dazzler.

perpetual repose awaits under a shade of cocoa palms, and tamarind trees, with a car-

pet of exquisite flowers variegating the " long
and pleasant grass." Euphorbiæ, passion flowers and great scarlet cacti, seem out of
place though, in the quiet God's-acre where
one has been accustomed to see " the violets
of his native land," but the sleepers here
have a further glory, their graves being
banked up with hugh conch shells, each with its
pink grinning mouth turned outwards, which
has a sufficiently fantastic effect.

During the morning, we paid a visit to the
harmless fort which acropolizes the town. It
is mounted with wonderful old cannon, and
commanded by a most agreeable and witty
major, who received us with great politeness.
I regret very much not having been to " Bu-
lowsminde," an old Governor's residence on the
heights, so prettily described by M. E. W. S.
in one of her stories ; but some little repairs
being needed for the schooner, we must hasten
to St. Thomas.

Horror! horror! *musquitoes!!*—they sing
as loud as bull frogs, bite like serpents, and
have appeared among us with the suddenness
of one of Pharoah's plagues.

November 24*th.*—After warping out past the
fort, we pass through the great coral barrier
and its pensive pelicans, who hardly take the
trouble to lift their absurd, over-grown heads
as we run by. The pilot steps into his boat,
and we are once more in blue water, heeling
over to the fresh easterly breeze, and bound
for St. Thomas.

We made the run of forty miles in four hours
and a half, notwithstanding three unpleasant
rain squalls, and now lie at anchor in the harbor
of Charlotte-Amalia, the capital of the island,
which, however, is only fifteen miles long,
and is a mass of rocks, without forests or much
low ground. The approach to the island
reminds one of Marblehead, and the entrance
to the harbor is exceedingly beautiful and
picturesque. It is narrow, but as we rushed
in, regardless of pilots, it widened into a lovely
bay, surrounded by a range of high hills
sloping to the water, and with their dome-like
summits rising 700 to 1,400 feet. The town
lies at their feet, built on three spurs of the
hills, and is a very gay looking place, the
streets rising in terraces, one above the other,

while the red-tiled roofs glitter in the clear atmosphere. The harbor is filled with ship-

Town and Harbor of St. Thomas.

ping, the wharves are crowded with boats, and the streets with niggers of every hue and expression, all chattering and leaping about surprisingly. I don't wonder the old buccaneers made this place the base of their piratical operations. It is full of neat little hiding places for vessels, and I looked with interest on the two towers, or rather their remains—

2*

one called Bluebeard's Tower, and the other Blackbeard's Tower—where these mild-mannered gentlemen used to lark and carouse after a successful expedition, and also "stow their swag." Bluebeard I only remember as a fanatical matrimonialist, but Blackbeard's cruel exploits are celebrated all through the islands. His mantle appears to have degenerately fallen upon the shopkeepers of the town.

The cool land breeze enjoyed on the deck of the tidy little "Josephine," is pleasanter than strolling about the up-and-down, sun-baked streets of the town; and then one gets so tired of the inevitable nigger. In this place, the females largely predominate in every hue and form of hideousness—yet they seem to have a patron or "touter," the vilest of niggers, who, though possessing the virtuous name of Snowball, haunted us in the streets with a wish to be our guide, philosopher, and friend. Nor could he be entirely got rid of.

November 25th.—Thank Heaven! the mosquitoes, or moschettos, as Humboldt calls them, (I wonder which is right,) have been killed or

blown away, and we are anchored just **far
enough** from land **to** prevent **their** getting **off**
to us. Their visit seems like a " dem'd **horrid
dream."** I visited Mr. Palgrave, **the British**
Consul, a very good fellow, **who appears to**
have got himself into a scrape by writing a clever
article in the *Cornhill* about **St. Thomas, in**
consequence of which he is execrated **by the**
inhabitants, on the principle, I fancy, **of** *" ce
n'est que la verité qui offense."* **The said**
inhabitants (there are no natives) are **composed**
of every race under the sun, and largely **flav-**
ored with **the** Hebrew **of Germany.** No one
seems to **be settled.** As each makes a com-
petence or **a** fortune, he shakes **off the dust of**
St. Thomas, and returns **to his native land.**

We were inscribed at **the Club, and found it
a** very comfortable place, on **a high** terrace
above the port, the windows and cool balcony
commanding a wonderful view of the **harbor,**
bay, and surrounding islands. **This is a very
busy port.** Shipping and steamers, large and
small, **are** constantly **arriving or departing,
while** multitudes of small **nigger-propelled
boats** are always to be seen darting **about.**

We have been carefully warned about bathing, as the harbor is full of sharks, and we have
two large shark-hooks baited, consequently,
over the taffrail. The beasts float gently up,
swallow the lump of beef, and then, finding
the hook inconvenient, bend it out straight,
and depart in peace—with the beef—so that
we have not yet captured one. We get daily
supplies, however, of delicious little fish, either
mullet or snappers, of all colors of the rainbow—red or spotted, or striped with gold—and
costing a mere trifle.

November 26*th.*—We have lovely days, with
a very hot vertical sun, but tempered by the
cool breath of the trade wind, until 4 o'clock,
when the breeze dies out, and till six the air is
very sultry and trying. The nights are filled with
music in the shape of rain-squalls, which come
down with violent regularity, splashing through
the skylights, and clattering down the wind-
sails, and either wet us all below, or oblige us to
take a Turkish bath by shutting up the cabin
tightly; however, the planters say that it is
magnificent weather for the cane. King Cane

reigns as paramount in the West Indies as King Cotton in the Southern States ; he regulates the wealth of all, and what is worse, he rules the conversation. Where two or three are gathered together I can be sure they are talking " Cane," and I carefully pass by on the other side.

There has been a great excitement in the town to-day over a species of "phillіloo," or Irish warfare, among the niggers, numbers of whom have been conveyed kicking to the Fort, and the row had to be suppressed by a party of the Danish garrison. I discovered that it was an annual occurrence. Christmas is approaching, and it seems that the colored population have a little way of beginning to keep it *early.* These same colored people seem, at any rate in the Danish islands, to have a higher range of intelligence than with us. Clerks in the custom house and government offices, book-keepers, store-keepers, bank clerks, are all niggers, and to-day we were " interviewed" on board, by two bright looking darkies, reporters for *the* newspaper. To-night the Governor holds his weekly reception, but the inclination to go is wanting, as we were naïvely informed by an official that the element of ladies was very deficient indeed, at these entertainments, owing to the fact that nearly all of these charmers are either having babies, or attending to their nursery duties. This is a growing colony!

November 27th.—To-day is almost a *dies non.* We swing lazily at our anchor, watching the incoming and outgoing vessels, and anxiously hoping for the arrival of a tardy *blanch*isseuse, that we may once more try the bounding billows to-morrow.

November 28th.—This morning we took in provisions, water, and ice, (the latter four cents per lb.,) preparatory to sailing; we had previously supplied ourselves with thin ready-made clothing, which St. Thomas supplies very cheaply to all the other islands, being a free port of entry, and L—— procured a wonderful tropical hat which made him look like an animated mushroom. With "a madness of farewells," K—— and R—— departed on shore with all their belongings, as they leave us here to return to New York. The mainsail is once more hoisted, the anchor comes home, and at noon we sail out of the harbor bound for Guadaloupe. C—— and I still remain with L——, to com-

Our Blanchisseuse.

plete the cruise, of which the most enjoyable part is yet to come.

As soon as we clear the islands, we bounce into a heavy sea with the wind dead ahead, so that we may be some time making the 240 miles that separate us from our destination. I cannot say that diving into a head sea, under double reefs and bonnet off the staysail, with water flying all over us, is quite the most comfortable condition for the quiet enjoyment of dinner.

November 29th.—We have weathered the shoals off the east end of Santa Cruz during the night, and are now speeding along within two points of our course, under full canvas, with a strong current against us. About 8 A. M., we sighted the singular island of Saba, and kept it in sight until nearly sundown, although we were averaging seven knots. This remarkable island is simply a volcano, rising abruptly out of the sea to a sugar-loaf elevation of about 3,000 feet; it is nearly round and about two miles across. It is inhabited by about 800 Dutchmen and their emancipated slaves. It is rather a difficult place to visit, as the tourist has to be hauled up the face of the rock in a basket, the inhabited spot being nearly a thousand feet up, and *lucus à non lucendo* it is called, "The Bottom;" singularly enough, the inhabitants are celebrated as the best boat builders and sailors in the West Indies; while in conse

Island of Saba.

quence of their lofty position they have a temperate climate and grow all European fruits and vegetables. As we passed this strange mountain, we ran across Saba Bank, a bed of living coral, in about ten fathoms of water, and we could plainly see the beautiful bottom and the fish darting about, while the water had the same sheeny satin effects that we noticed off Porto Rico. To-day has been our most beautiful

tropical day yet, a moderate sea and a fine even
breeze made sailing delightful, and the sunset
was a marvel of splendor,—it illustrated Sir
Walter Scott.

> " And now my guilty course is run,
>   Mine be the eve of tropic sun
>   No pale gradations quench his ray,
>   No twilight dews his wrath allay;
>   With disc like battle-target red
>   He rushes to his fiery bed,
>   Dyes the wild wave with bloody light—
>   Then sinks at once—and all is night."

November 30th.—At daylight, with a smooth
sea and very little wind, we make land right
ahead to the S. E., and by noon we were about
thirty miles from Basse Terre, the capital of
Guadaloupe. We have, also, to feast our curious eyes, on the horizon, the twin mountains
of Montserrat, a cluster of islands and rocky
peaks called " les Saintes," just south of Guadaloupe and farther to the southward the great
mountain of Dominica, called Morne Diablotin,
4,747 feet high, rears his dark head in the distance—but alas!

> " The best laid plots of mice and men
>   Gang aft agley."

At this time a stark flat calm fell upon us; **all**
day our sails flapped in the heavy ocean swell,
the **sun shot** down his **very** hottest **and most**
vertical rays, and it was evidently all up with
the wonderfully short run which we were going
to make **to** Guadaloupe. We possessed our
souls with patience, refreshed our bodies with
" cabin stores," and amused ourselves with **the**
performances of a shark, which darted **round**
the boat, making beautiful rays in the clear
blue water. I threw over **a** hook weighted with
a pound of beef, and it lay far below the surface, glittering like a living malachite, **until**
the clever beastie ate off all the beef and **retir-**
ed. A squall of wind and rain coming up, we
lost sight of him, and about dark the regular
sea breeze set in again, so that we are approaching the coast under easy sail.

December 1*st.*—This has been a day of disappointment and yawning. All day we have
been gently heaving on the long ocean swell
our sails idly " slatting " in a flat calm, within
ten miles of our Canaan ; and we **are out of
lemons ; not an** orange left in the locker. **The**

island of Guadaloupe is undoubtedly before us, and we should be able to enjoy its panorama of mountain and of valley, were it not for an envious cloud that clothes and almost conceals the whole shore. It occasionally sends off a visitor to us in the shape of a heavy rain squall, but the main body sits immovable on the mountains. There is something contemptible in a calm—the majesty of ocean disappears— his mighty waves become mere wrinkles, and the distant islands, at other times ringed with surf, just glimmer like gray ghosts through the hot and hazy atmosphere.

December 2*d.*—I really despaired this morning, when I came on deck, and saw by the pale glimmer of the waning moon, that we were still idly tossing about, ten miles from land, and without a breath of air to fan the uncertain sails. Before us, grim and dark, towered the great Souffrière, 5,500 feet above the sea level, surrounded by fantastic mountain peaks piled pyramid on pyramid, and as I looked, a white streak of dawn sharpened each outline, and deepened the shadow under the savage lava-worn lip of the crater. Peak after peak defined its clear, bold shape against the increasing light

> "And on the glimmering limit far withdrawn
> God made himself an awful rose of dawn."

I say peak after peak, because we are on the western, or Carribean side of Guadaloupe; which really consists of two islands separated by a narrow river; and while the eastern island is flat and sandy this western side rises from the ocean in one lofty, grand, volcanic mass, containing upwards of fourteen craters (probably extinct) and ranging upward, higher and higher, towards the southern end, divided by gullies hundreds of feet in depth, each peak tinged with rainbow lights or glittering in the sun's rays—

> "While all the glens are drowned in azure gloom."

The monarch of all is the Souffrière (which name however is given to the volcanoes on many other islands). His summit, or crater, is generally concealed by clouds and vapor, but

I have twice had the good fortune to see his frowns unveiled. He has been quiet now since his great eruption of 1797; but in 1843, he let himself off in an earthquake which destroyed the whole town of Point à Pitre (on the eastern island) and at intervals now he sends out occasional warnings of flame and smoke to intimate what he will do the next time he gets ready. At his foot in a beautiful bay lies the picturesque little town of Basse Terre close to which we have been quietly anchored, while I have been writing, having at last succeeded in getting in before nightfall. A delicious coolness steals down upon us from the mountains; very agreeable after two days of horrid and torrid calms.

"At last," as Mr. Kingsley says, we are anchored in the old citadel of the fierce and warlike Caribs, who controlled the whole semicircle of islands, from Porto Rico to Trinidad, according to Washington Irving, and it was from this place that they made their savage expeditions, and procured provisions for their cannibal entertainments. Columbus described in 1493 the very Souffrière at whose base we are peacefully lying, with no fear of any worse savages than the bloodthirsty musquitoes, and although dusky forms, crowding in canoes, hover round us, offering to barter—their propositions are eminently peaceful, and, in some cases, more than civilized.

December 3d.—Basse Terre is a long, straggly town, built along the beach, and the walls of the houses rise out of the water. It is a fearfully dull place, and with the exception of a few shops kept by white French people, we see nothing but low built houses, tenanted by the colored race, and we meet none but niggers, each with his burden

Negro Porters.

on his head. West Indian niggers invariably carry their loads in this way, from a box of

wine or a tray of cocoa-nuts, down to a demi-
john or a bottle of medicine, their style of dress
not including a possible side pocket. We landed at a very pretty " place " or square, shaded
with tamarind trees, and the town is refreshed
and kept clean by plenty of mountain streams
rushing down across the streets, but alas !
how changed from their spring-like purity before they reach the sea, only those know who
have been anchored near them.

The largest of these streams bisects the town,
and from the bridge we beheld clusters of almost naked negresses performing the rite of
(what they fondly call) washing. They simply
dabble the linen in the stream, and then laying
it on a pointed rock, beat it viciously with another equally sharply angled, until it is reduced to a pulp. The shirt when returned to its
owner, presents the appearance of very irregu-
lar lace. A stroll in the market place brought
us among crowds of clamorous negresses, rather
more clothed than their naiad sisters, each sitting behind heaps of beautiful fruits, vegetables,
and brilliant colored fish, and each prepared to
cheat us out of as many francs as possible.

Among them were some Hindoo coolie women, with what an Irishman might call earrings in their noses. Our chief desire was to ascend the Souffrière, but we tried in vain, with the help of the English consul, to get quadrupeds to carry us up—to all suggestions and prayers "*Jamain joudui peute demain*" was the ridiculous *patois* answer, which we presumed meant "don't see it to-day, perhaps to-morrow"—so we accepted, instead, the consul's kind invitation to breakfast.

Family Matters.

He lives in a funny little back slum with a stream of doubtful water running down the

3

middle of it, and here and there a group of colored persons dabbling in it, and gabbling their soft-sounding *patois* without a break: but the house and garden were charming, and the repast a collection of the most surprising and delicious fruits—oranges, mangoes, sapadilla, avocado, grenadilla figs, vied with each other in temptation, and above all an exquisite little fruit called " pomme de liane." It is about the size of a sickel pear, color and rind like a ripe pumpkin, and I could never have blamed Adam, if our first mother had tempted him with a nice ripe one. We took leave of our entertainer with thanks for the repast, but with great fears for the immediate future, as no mortal from the north could withstand such fruits, yet no calamity overtook us.

To my great regret I could obtain no photographs of the beautiful scenery of the island, and we took advantage of the evening land breeze to depart from the deadly, lively place, bound for Martinique.

December 4th.—We carried a fine breeze with us till midnight, and then fell into a disheartening sail rendering calm, which lasted till noon, so that we only just succeeded in reaching St. Pierre, the capital of Martinique, by sundown. Each island that we approach seems lovelier than the last. To-day we ran by the island of Dominica and its wild chain of lofty mountains, which from being densely wooded have a dark and gloomy appearance; but Martinique, as we see it from the sea, is certainly the loveliest island we have yet beheld. The usual boatload of niggers comes alongside, and the blackest and most toothless of them is the pilot, under whose guidance we beat into the open roadstead which represents the harbor of St. Pierre, and gliding under the shadow of Mount Peleé, a threatening monster of a volcano, we make fast to the government moorings near the shore of the very pretty town over which he presides, and sometimes threatens, as in 1851, when he suddenly burst out with smoke and flames, and covered the island with ashes, scaring the inhabitants out of their wits.

The high *coteaux* are lovely with the contrasts of bright green sugar cane, dark coffee plantations, and variegated forests towered over by lofty palms, which shoot up a hundred feet or so before they spread their feathery coronal, and dotted over the landscape are the *usines* or sugar estates with their white buildings and tall chimneys. The port contains a large number of vessels which, owing to the great depth of water in the roads, are anchored close in shore, and also moored by the stern, a process we shall have to undergo to-morrow morning. The town looks very gay from our deck; but we resist its blandishments till to-morrow.

December 5th.—A great deal of shouting and struggling brought us to our anchorage, and we have at last got our stern moorings made fast ashore, all right. The town is very handsome, and the houses well built of stone, which gives the place a sort of provincial French air. The streets are terraced above each other in an up and down way, and one comes quite suddenly upon unexpected and very steep hills. The market place is spacious, and usually filled with the jabbering crowd of niggers, who look as if they had suddenly reappeared from Guadaloupe, to have another look at us. There is also the same watercourse dividing the town, and the same bridge from which we again beheld at least a hundred black females offering up sacri-

Lace-Making.

fices of linen. We received a great deal of politeness and attention from the British consul, Mr. Lawless, who walked around with us to point out the lions, showed us the Bishop's garden and introduced us to the Cercle Privée, or club.

After our return on board, we had a mild imitation of a chapter from the "Earl and the Doctor," in the shape of a visitation of many mulattoes, *des deux* sexes, apparently as bare as robins, who swarmed about round us, and dived with great agility for half-francs which they invariably caught, and stowed away in their mouths. These primitive little games became tiresome though, as our half-francs diminished —and as it seemed to be a thing that went on all day, our principles were not dangerously undermined.

December 6th.—To-day being Sunday we attended High Mass in the Cathedral, which is a large but not imposing edifice—and although they have a good sized organ, they do not use it, but seem to prefer a sort of harmonium near the altar. The congregation was, of course, of all hues except white. The ladies all knelt on their own little carpets and cushions in the centre aisle, and many of them were very pretty. The shops were kept religiously shut during church-time, but were reopened afterwards, and the streets were very gay with the crowds of holiday keepers. In the afternoon we walked to the Savanna, a large, open space beyond the town, and the favorite promenade of the St. Pierrots; beyond this, again, we found the Botanical Gardens, beautifully laid

out with a very good collection of tropical trees
and orchids, besides many varieties of palms,

The Ceiba Tree.

an immense poinsettia in full scarlet glory—
I thought the most splendid plant I ever beheld—so different from the feeble shrubs one

sees in the northern greenhouses. A very pretty lake stands in the centre of the gardens, and supports a large variety of aquatic plants, but perhaps the glory of the place is an enormous Ceiba or silk cotton tree, whose immense branches have probably shaded many a cannibal repast prepared under its curious buttressed trunk.

They have a museum, too, containing specimens of all the indigenous beasts, birds and fishes, and particularly snakes, which infest the island most uncomfortably. There is a fellow called the *Fer de lance*, a yellow snake with a tail like a rat, a very ugly customer to meet, and dreaded by the laborers and field hands. About 150 people died of snake bites last year. It was very pleasant to turn from such nasty things, back to the Savanna, where the whole population appeared to be walking in their Sunday clothes. Then I saw the real Martinique beauties. Oh! how lovely they are! such pretty feet and hands, lithe graceful, undulating figures, and flashing saucy eyes, under a jaunty red or yellow silk tokyne, are to be seen nowhere else. And then how they dress! nowhere else

could they venture on the *Jupe de Martinique*,
which is simply a piece of showy stuff wound
or draped round the body for a skirt, but so
draped, and worn with such a *démarche*,
Vera incessu patuit Dea! they are very
charming. The British Consul returned on
board, and dined with us. I could not
but admire his courage; we sat in the
cabin with the mercury at 85°, perspiring
freely in our shirt sleeves, while he never
unbuttoned his blue and buttony uniform, and
he never turned a hair.

December 7th.—This morning, Mr. Lawless
having very kindly provided us with horses, a
guide, and a spur apiece, we started away
before sunrise, to "*les Eaux chaudes*," or as
the proprietor, with much dignity calls it,
"*L'Etablissement bes Bains Thermo-mineraux
du Prêchuer.*" It lies up the mountain some
ten miles from St. Pierre; our road, for the
first four miles, lay by the side of the ocean,
through delicious shady groves, of cocoa palms,
tamarinds, ceiba, and mangoes, by little farms,
fields of cane, and pretty embowered villages,

each with its little wayside shrine and rude image of the Mater Dolorosa, or Salvator mundi, a devout worshipper or two, and bunches of faded flower offerings on the steps. We see these everywhere, and none of the many market people we meet trudging to the town with loads of vegetables or fruit, pass them without at least crossing themselves.

My Steed.

Our way suddenly diverged into a little mountain bridle path, where ascending single file, between masses of verdure and a wilderness of blooms which fill the air with sweetness, and fording the many clear little torrents that gush out of the scarred old flanks of Peleus, our sure-footed little beasts, at last brought us to a large plateau about 500 feet above the level of the sea, and from which we had the most exquisite view of ocean, wild mountain, and wilder ravine. Here stands the *Etablisse-ment*, which is simply a wooden structure with galleries all about it, with all but the lower story open to the four winds of Heaven, the upper part being used for drying cocoa beans. Our long hot ride made the prospect of a bath peculiarly grateful, but I never can describe the complete splendor and delight of *that* bath. We hurriedly arranged for a little breakfast, and then, conducted by a mulatto goddess, entered a long shed under which is the place of delight, a long brick-paved, very clean place, large enough for one to take seven or eight swimming strokes, and filled with the mineral water to the depth of five feet. The water is of the Vichy order and tastes quite alkaline, and is of the temperature of new milk. How we plunged into it again and again! how we revelled in it, and staying in it nearly an hour, came out like John Bunyan, after his pack rolled away from him, invigorated, refreshed, and oh! how hungry! We sauntered back to the house to breakfast, and I draw a discreet veil over the quantity of *omelettes-au-lant* that we made away with. We met an intelligent young *padre*, so much younger than myself that it seemed a lark to call him "*mon Père*," and a neighboring *propriètaire* with whom we shared our *Pommeraye sec*, and discoursed of many things during the hour or two of gentle languor and cigars, that came like the reward of a good action. Altogether it was an enchanting excursion, but our last one here, for to my regret, L—— decided to get under weigh for Barbadoes, with the land breeze this evening, so we bid a sad farewell to the enchantments and attractions of this loveliest of the Antilles. Good-bye, dear Martinique, I don't think we shall meet with anything better.

> "The cloud may stoop from heaven and take the shape,
>   With fold to fold, of mountain or of cape,"

but cannot surpass my Martinique.

I have tried, but not very successfully, to

collogue with the natives in their horrid *patois*. It seems to be a jargon based on the French, and composed of sounds and corruptions of words, that fit most naturally to the nigger organs of speech. It is a very undignified, toothless sort of dialect, soft, but silly in the extreme. The natives love it best though, and although they will speak French if you insist, the rascals will always try to draw you into their ridiculous gabble.

December 8th.—After baffling about under short sail all night, we found ourselves this morning at the southern end of Martinique, and close to the celebrated Diamond Rock, which rises six hundred feet clean out of the water, is only about a mile round, and was considered unclimbable until Admiral Hood, in 1804, made a hawser fast to the top from his ship, "The Centaur," and succeeded in hauling up five guns, which were placed in position, and defended by 120 men with four months' provisions. The rock was actually rated on the admiralty books as H. M. S. Diamond Rock, and the position was held for a year and a half, until for want of powder, it was surrendered to the French squadron. It is astonishing to think of the tremendous fights that have taken place over these West India Islands, and the quantity of lives that have been spent in the various changes of ownership that each has undergone. On our starboard hand is the beautiful but snaky island of St. Lucia, also the scene of some very hard fighting. It is towered over by the singular twin mountains at its western end, called the Pitons, which, about a mile apart, rush sheer out of the sea up about 3,000 feet, are covered with heavy woods, and quite inaccessible. There is a story of some sailors trying to climb one of them, and being all killed by the *fer de lance*. Behind them is a lovely little bay, bathing the foot of the fantastic Souffrière, now of rather diminished loftiness, having blown his own crater all to pieces in the last eruption. As we catch a favoring breeze, we soon leave these beautiful islands behind us, getting, however, a distant view of St. Vincent and his big volcanic peak. All the evening we bowl along about nine knots an hour towards Barbadoes. One among us had been observed violently sucking a stump of black lead pencil during the day, and asking the steward for note paper. So no one was surprised when, the cloth being removed and cigars lighted, our conversation took this kind of form:

T.—"Look here! the buccaneerishness of these latitudes has awakened the deep well of poetry I have always thought was hidden within me. I yearn for the unattainable. I have burst into song. Now just give me, both of you, your opinion on this little thing. I call it rather neat—but mind, it's copyrighted. You are not to go sending it to the girl you left behind you as a tenderness of your own."

(*L*—— *disappears hastily up the companionway.*)

"Never mind. C—— *you* have a soul for this sort of thing, just listen and be thrilled!

> " **Far** 'neath the tropic sky, our wandering barque
> **Rises** upon the rolling purple wave,
> **The sun, low** on the confines of the dark,
> **Seems in** the **deep** his burning disc to lave.
> **As flies** the white **foam** o'er the crested sea,
> **So fly my** burning thoughts, **O Love, to thee!**"

L. (*on deck.*)—" Clew down the maintopsail, and furl it. Stand by foresail halliards."

C.—" There! I knew such rot would bring a squall! Oh dear, I thought one might have 'ust one quiet night too—everything acts just ike the devil!"

> T.—   " Vex not thou the poet's mind
>   With thy shallow wit,

but listen to the splendid effect of the next stanza."

C.—" Patience is a virtue. Steward! some brandy and water."

> T.—   " A speck upon the heaving ocean's breast,
>   The compass guides our trackless path aright,
>   But my unquiet heart, in wild unrest,
>   Yearns with its weight of love throughout the
>   night !
>   The perfumed south wind speeds us o'er the sea,
>   And all my soul is full, O Love, of thee ! "

L. (*on deck.*)—" Lower away foresail, handsomely now! Call starboard watch, and reef mainsail."

C.— " Serves us right! your perfumed south wind is going to give us fits, and while they are reefing I should like to know how your what's-his-name heart, in wild thingammy, **is** like our steady-going old compass. Shut up and take some of this."

T.—" You have no poetry in your soul. I shall turn in."

December 9th.—We made such good time in the night, that we had to heave-to off the coast and wait **till** daylight. The morning sun **was** just turning the hill palms to gold, as we filled away and sailed into **the** harbor of Bridgetown, **the** capital **of** Barbadoes. This island, as **seen** from **the** sea, is quite different from any other **of** the islands we have visited, the difference is that of a quiet respectable citizen from a wild and dazzling pirate. Here in Barbadoes are no volcanoes **or** souffrières to hold the island **in** awe, no wild forests, or savage peaks with dee**p** azure glens and ravines; all is smooth, quiet, snug, highly cultivated and densely populated; even nature seems controlled by the spirit **of** British respectability, and at **a** distance, were **it** not for **the** palm-trees, one might imagine one**'s** self sailing up to the Isle **of** Wight. The population **is remarkable,** being **over** 162,000 for

3*

an island eighteen miles long by twelve miles broad, and we saw very unfavorable specimens of it as we ran into the harbor, in the shape of immense numbers of most persevering and repulsive darkies who flocked round us in small boats, keeping up with us as we shortened sail, offering quite unnecessary pilotage and screaming out most injurious statements about each other and each other's family relations. We had absolutely to obtain the assistance of the harbor police to clear them off, having with the greatest difficulty prevented them from swarming all over the schooner, until we finally dropped anchor some distance from the wharf landing, outside the mole, and near an English corvette, the "Druid."

As soon as we landed we were assailed by a cloud of pestiferous niggers *des deux sexes*, who hovered round us like musquitos, except that the sense they offended was not that of touch, and while endeavoring to drive them off, we were reinforced by a New Yorker whom I had known under less trying circumstances, and eventually succeeded in reaching the Ice House, which is the café and general supply store of

the town.   Here we met the U. S. consul and
went through a liberal course of introductions,

Street Scene in Bridgetown.

making the acquaintance also of a voluminous
but enticing drink known as "swizzle."   Our

friend very kindly lent us his carriage, in which we proceeded to pay our respects to the Governor of the Windward Islands, Hon. Rawson W. Rawson, to whom we had a letter of introduction. Government House is about a mile out of town, and stands in the midst of a perfect paradise of most beautiful gardens. The Governor, whose scientific tastes are well known, showed us his collection of shells and marine curiosities, which Mr. Agassiz pronounced to be the most perfect he had seen, and after a pleasant conchological hour we visited the gardens where my ignorance, I hope, was less conspicuous. The botanical collection was admirable, and it seemed charming to have a greenhouse without the northern appliances of glass and stoves. I forbear a list of nomenclatures of the lovely things I saw, feeling that the splendid tree fern is not more admirable when called *Polypodium arboreum.* We wound up at the very nice club in the town, so that we may be said to be free of the city, and the hospitable people seem to think they can't do enough to make it pleasant for us. The town itself is very British and substantial, and the environs are rows of pretty houses and gardens reminding one, *mutatis mutandis*, of St. John's Wood. With a little more breeze and a good many less niggers, it would be delightful.

December 10*th*.—We have been lying quietly at anchor all day, enjoying a repose heightened by the certainty that everybody must be very hot ashore. The weather is too trying until nearly sundown. We went ashore in the evening, and drove round the pleasant outskirts of the town to a suburb called Hastings, which is prettily situated on a coral point, and contains the houses of most of the European residents, also the barracks, parade ground, and an ominous monument erected to the victims of the hurricane of 1831, which seems to have been very destructive, over 2000 people having lost their lives.

December 11*th*.—To-day has very much resembled yesterday, the same visits from hopeful *blanchiseuses* (badly named, for they all vie with the ace of spades) and bumboat women, and a great many friendly visitations from residents of the place. One gentleman lent us his carriage for a very pleasant drive among the cane-fields and by the sea shore; another gave us a charming evening at his house, where we made the acquaintance of a bowl of Barbadian punch, the ingredients of which I here give to a grateful world: Holland gin, sugar, limes, fresh cocoanut milk, and ice. I have no expression strong enough to describe my entire respect for it.

While we were in Martinique we bought a brace of green turtles for four dollars, and these succulent creatures, each with a hole through his shell and a long painter, enjoy themselves in their native element awaiting their final destiny. Their lives have been prolonged from the fact that the Ice House supplies us with perfect turtle soup, composed really of turtle, and not strengthened with beef and veal stock, such as we know of in the North. L—— has some cases of Sercial Madeira, too, which that clever old connoisseur Coleridge, who visited the islands forty years ago, says is the true wine for turtle—and how right he is!

December 12*th*.—We landed this morning to take breakfast with Mr. P——, a merchant of the place. His pretty residence surrounded by mahogany trees, was at some distance from the town, as indeed everybody's appears to be, and I enjoyed the sight of a collection of tropical ferns, such as could hardly be assembled in temperate zones. We met with a singularly good *plat* at this entertainment, being the roes of flying fish scrambled with eggs. How nice it sounds! and it tastes even better. The flying-fish is quite an article of food here, as immense quantities are netted round the island by the trim, cranky-looking little boats with large sails that one sees cruising about in the offing. After a *siesta* we went ashore again to a dinner-party at Government House. Every man was in uniform but ourselves, and our black coats *faisaient tâche* in the general effect. The charming presence of the ladies was, if possible, the more agreeable to us after a long absence from home, and the perpetual haranguing of blackies, and I was sorry when the "governess" gave that mysterious signal for departure that always ends the very best of dinners. Everybody seemed so kind, friendly and hospitable, that a winter passed here could not but be very pleasant. The only great objection to Barbadoes is the tremendous *cheek* and insolence of the " Bim " as the nigger of the island is called. No one could believe it possible, or appreciate it unless he had suffered and endeavored to endure it. The Book of Job would never have been written, had that interesting sufferer lived in Barbadoes.

December 13*th.*—A delightful day of *far niente.* We literally did nothing, with the exception of a visit to the officers of the 97th in barracks, who were as hospitable as everybody else.

December 14*th.*—A very busy, happy day indeed. We were ashore by seven o'clock, to enjoy an excursion which had been arranged for us by some of our polite entertainers to the east or windward side of the island. We found their carriages waiting for us and off we started over the capital coral roads, (the entire island being nothing but a coral formation) glittering and white, through endless plantations of the now rather wearisome sugar-cane for about sixteen miles, when we halted on the edge of a long abrupt cliff, about seven hundred feet high, and suddenly beheld one of the most exquisite views the eye ever rested on. Beneath us was unrolled a wide panorama of cultivated fields, avenues of palms, houses, huts, a church or two, a lighthouse, and on the verge the white surf of the Atlantic restlessly rolling upon the coral beach. I believe this part of the island is called Scotland, perhaps from a fancied resemblance to the Trosachs. After enjoying the view to the utmost, we drove about a mile further to St. John's church, the oldest on the island, where, after moralizing in the old churchyard, we partook of a slight repast in the vestry. We got back to Bridgetown shortly after noon, rather exhausted with the hot sun, but found that our entertainers had prepared another gorgeous repast at the club, to which we did what honor we could. We spent our afternoon in receiving visits until it was time for us to go on board the Prussian brig of war " Undine," where we were invited to dine. The officers were a capital set of fellows, and gave us an excellent dinner in the ward room. I was put next the chaplain, as he couldn't speak a word of English and the other officers all could more or less, and a very jolly companion he was. The chief ornaments of the ward room were a cask of Rudesheimer and one of Steinberger neatly stowed in different corners. It was like Mrs. Chickenstalker's "notion of a little flip," and it was pleasant to know that we had so much to fall back upon, for never was the generous growth of the Rhine more thoroughly appreciated; indeed we subsequently restored one young guest to his family, of whom it could be said, *abiit, excessit, erupit, evasit,*—in English— he went out to dinner, he took more hock than was good for him—he had a tremendous spree —*he said it was the salmon.*

The "Undine" being a school ship, had lots of boys on board, and after dinner they all sang quantities of German songs, very prettily indeed. Still, it was not disagreeable at last to step into the gig and return to our own quarters and repose, for no one can deny that the two most fatiguing exertions in life are sight-seeing and dinner-parties.

December 15*th.*—Chastened but not discouraged, the morning sun finds us after yesterday's exercises. We paid a quantity of "farewellers" and regretfully declined many invitations, L—— having decided to get underway this afternoon for Trinidad, as it is desirable to sight the island of Tobago, which lies directly in our route, at daylight to-morrow. We left all the Barbadians preparing for a grand ball at the barracks, and stood gallantly out of the harbor. About midnight I saw the wonderful phosphorescence of the water described by Humboldt, as we rapidly slipped through it with a fair wind. The moon had just set and the crest of every wave was aflame; the lines towing astern with the patent logs, were serpents of living fire, and all the sea where we cleft it with our prow or left it seething in our wake, seemed boiling flames.

December 16*th.*—At daylight we sighted the island of Tobago, and gradually as we drew nearer, its lofty peaks and deep chasm—like valleys covered with forest, became distinct, but not even the glow of morning sun could

destroy the dismal, uninhabited look of the
island. The appearance of the lofty, gloomy
mountains and black precipices, descending
abruptly to the sea, have caused it to be most
appropriately called "The Melancholy Isle."
It has a peculiar interest as the island on which
"poor Robinson Crusoe" was cast away, and
as we passed its southern point and saw the
surf rolling upon its desolate sands, one could
imagine the startling footprint and the Caribs
landing from the neighboring island of Trinidad : in fact we beheld the little " cove running
up inland and the heavy swell on the beach."
As we run past, the lofty range of mountains on
the north coast of Trinidad comes in sight on the
horizon, shrouded in mist and rain-squalls, and
at sundown we heave-to, being unable to pass
the rough entrance to the Gulf of Paria till daylight.

December 17*th*.—With a fresh breeze we
filled away at daylight for the Bocas de
Dragone—the Dragon's Mouths—which are the
narrow entrances by the north to the beautiful
Gulf of Paria, the great embouchure of the

Oronoco, whose mighty waters tinge the gulf a muddy bottle-green color, very different from the delightful Mediterranean-blue of the Caribbean Sea. The gulf is a great harbor, affording

The Dragon's Mouths.

anchorage in every part, ninety miles long, and forty-five miles wide, completely land-locked, the only other issue but that we are approaching being the entrance at the southern point of Trinidad, and agreeably named Boca del Sierpe—the Serpent's Mouth—where Columbus had a very serious scare. The water may be called fresh, to distinguish it from the salt of the sea, but it is not nice for drinking, and rather unpromising for bathing purposes. The bay is a "dolorous inland sea," land-locked by the island of Trinidad on the east, and the main land of Venezuela on the other. The main land! *Tierra firma!* This was the goal of the hopes of Columbus, of Raleigh and his great Elizabethan co-adventurers. Here were the scenes of the matchless history of Amyas Lee. We are now merrily sliding through the laughing sea where nearly four hundred years ago the little caravels of the discoverer for the first time bore him towards "a fair and beautiful coast, covered with stately forests," just as it is now. We pass between the lofty wooded cliffs, which, rising sheer from the sea, form the three "mouths" the Dragon affords to the navigator, and, finding ourselves almost becalmed under the great mountains, had a long opportunity of thoroughly enjoying the rich, luxuriant, wild and varied scenery that surrounded us. On one hand the mountains, valleys, and cultivated plains of Trinidad; on the other the high mountains of Cumana, crowned with vaporous fleecy clouds; savage, mysterious, and impenetrable; clothed from top to bottom with immense trees; the end of the great chain, according to Humboldt (*Ansichten der Natur*), of the Andes of Peru. These mountains end in a long cape, which is met by the mountains of Trinidad, the Bocas de Dragone lying between, and seem to prove Humboldt's belief that the island belongs to the shore of the continent, rather than to the system of the West India Islands. It is impossible to adequately describe the enchanting land and water views that opened before us as we slowly sailed along under the mountain's shadow, until late in the afternoon, when we cast anchor in the harbor of Port of Spain, the capital of the island, built at the foot of the mountains, on the ugly, flat, muddy shores of the gulf. The river Caroni pours out its filthy, crocodile-haunted waters just below the town, and forms a low, unhealthy delta of alluvium, covered with the disgusting mangrove trees. The site of the town is decidedly unprepossessing as seen from the harbor.

As we sit in the cool moonlight, on deck, I can't help thinking that hundreds of years before the Englishman came, scaring the Don into burning his great fleet, and took possession of this, the largest of the islands, a very lively kind of warfare was kept up by the savage aborigines. Notwithstanding the holy name given it by the Spanish explorers, Columbus had a very naïve method of bestowing the blessings of Chistianity upon his discoveries. He landed, planted a cross, called the place after some saint, perhaps said a mass, and then went on his way rejoicing. The new discovery had thus become Christian, which did not, however, seem to prevent them from killing and eating each other, just as before.

December 18*th*.—We landed early this morning to visit the town, which, though large, spacious, and busy, still retains the quaint Spanish appearance, which denotes its original ownership. We walked about under the guidance of the consul, staring at the shops, and noticing the squalor and semi-nudity of the negro population. The British character never seems to amalgamate well with the African race, it appears to render them cross grained and hideous of aspect, while the combination of the French and the negro makes a delightful mixture—this I noticed particularly at Martinique. But the labor of this island is mostly carried on by Hindoo coolies, who form a very great and advantageous contrast to the indigenous darkey.

Coolies at Work.

They are a thin, lithe, long-haired, copper-colored people, very cleanly, with handsome delicate features, great deportment, and carefully preserving their Hindoo costume, if such slender

4

suggestions can be dignified by that name. The women, when not adorned with rings in their noses, are pretty, and wear gold and sil-

Coolie and Negro.

ver bangles, necklaces and anklets, and bracelets above the elbow; they also indulge in gorgeous but always harmonizing colors. The employment of this class is, I understand, still an experiment, but being intelligent and thrifty, they are gradually becoming proprietors in a small way, and seem much superior to the African, though without the enormous strength that the latter possesses.

The environs of the town are quite charming. All the handsomest residences surround the Savanna, which is the fashionable promenade, race course and parade ground, and we visited the Governor's houses and gardens, and some other exquisite gardens, all filled with the loveliest tropical trees and flowers. Here we met the bread-fruit tree and the mango; but the orchids were evidently the great pride of their owners, and yet they are simply collected from the forests or "high woods," as they are called.

We dined pleasantly with the consul and a medico from New York, who is at present wasting his sweetness on the coolies, though far too good a fellow to languish in these hot climes. The great trouble in yachting among these islands, lies in obtaining provisions—not vegetables, for the markets are crowded with them—nor fruit, for it abounds in infinite variety, lusciousness and cheapness—but meat is only obtained dripping from the freshly killed beast and must be eaten the same day. We modify the inconvenience a little by carrying live stock, such as chickens, ducks, pigeons, turkeys, etc., and our menagerie has now received the addition of two black pigs, (all pigs are black in the West Indies, probably from association) playful and ignorant of their fate:—they are rather beyond the white-souled innocence of the sucking pig, and yet are mere piglets or porkerines. The fishermen come alongside every morning bringing excellent little fish, and invariably try to tempt us with huge saurians, the very Gogs and Magogs of lobsters. The only edible game here is the *Lapo*, (the doctor has a live one in his back garden, but as a pet and not for domestic purposes). This queer creature is a compound of the hare, the beaver, and the tom-cat, yet is amphibious. It reminded me so of the "slithy toves" in "Jabberwock," that I couldn't touch it, but C—— said it wasn't very nasty.

December 19*th*.—A quiet morning on board with few visitors. In the afternoon we went up to the reservoir, a drive of four or five miles beyond the Savanna, through the most beautiful ravine densely wooded, and bordering the road with orange groves and plantations of cacao, interspersed with great copses of the " king of grasses," the graceful bamboo. The cacao, of which chocolate is made bears the gracious name of *Theobroma*, God's food, and is a very singular tree. Planted in rows, it bears a dense dark foliage through which glisten the long red and yellow pods of fruit, which also shoot out of the trunk or root, without the pretense of a twig or leaf near them. As the tree requires sun in winter and shade in summer, each row is alternated with a row of the *Bois Immortelle*, a beautiful lofty tree which conveniently leaves in the summer, and in winter is covered with large red blossoms only. These plantations which form the chief industry of the island, consequently add a richness and beauty indescribable, to the landscape. The town is surrounded by dreadful back slums where the colored people live, but the squalor

and filth are so palliated by the beautiful palms,
plantains, or tamarind trees that start up everywhere among them, that the nastiness of it all
does not strike one like the grim horrors of
Mackerelville or little Dublin. The streets are
haunted, too, by evil spirits, shrouded in the form
of the *corbeau,* a kind of turkey-buzzard, only

Foul Proceedings.

more so; they have a perpetual contract for the
offal of the town, and are allowed to roost all
over the houses; they are black, hideous and as
impudent as a Bim.

C—— came back later from an excursion in
the mountains with the Doctor, brimful of en-
thusiasm at the beauty of the scenery and the

beanty of the coolinas—especially the latter.
This, then, is the result of those deleterious
readings on the voyage down!

December 20*th.*—Early this morning we got
under way, and, accompanied by the most
obliging of consuls, Mr. Fulton Paul, sailed
about thirty miles down the coast to Point la
Brea, a long promontory on the west shore,
where the celebrated Pitch Lake is situated.
As we glided along through the smooth but
foul water, we had a capital view of the
detached cliffs of the Dragon's Mouths, where
the ocean first broke the rocky bulwark and
made an island of Trinidad. About noon we
landed by beaching the boat in a heavy surf,
which tumbled us all out in a ridiculous manner, and wetted us completely through.

The instant one lands, pitch prevails. The
pebbles even on the beach are pitch, and the
few inhabitants who came down to meet us
were pitchy, and of the color of that defiling
substance. We had about a mile to walk, accompanied by a guide and two niggers bearing
a pitchy plank, which was shortly to come into

play. I also carried my gun. Our road lay
between great banks of lovely flowers, roseaux,
and groo-groo palms. The day was perfectly
delightful, a fresh sea breeze tempering the
heat, and we went in for a regular school-boy
scamper.

The black surface of this extraordinary lake
is seamed in every direction with pools of
water and crevasses, some of great depth. The
shallow ones we waded through, and at the
deep ones the plank came into requisition.
Here and there from the black bosom of the
pitch rise small islets, covered with beautiful
trees, shrubs and flowers, tufts of wild pine-
apple and aloes, the trees ornamented with
bizarre orchids, and everywhere radiant butterflies, and birds of exquisite plumage, some of
which I shot, with wild ideas of taxidermy, and
afterwards greatly regretted the useless destruction of such brilliant creatures—the only
useful deaths were those of some plover—while
absurd birds like robins flew about us, shouting " *Qu'est qu'il dit, qu'est qu'il dit,*" from
which they are named.

L—— became imbued with a sportsman's

ardor, and taking the gun, with his eyes fixed on his prey, waded into a crevasse, and suddenly disappeared under water, waving the gun above the surface. Ten minutes on the hot pitch, however, dried his clothes. In the middle of the lake we found a large space, perhaps half an acre, of pitch, boiling and bubbling as if hot from the infernal cauldron, and at another spot we found the surface so hot as to be very uncomfortable even through our shoes, while the barefooted niggers were kept ridiculously leaping up and down like the celebrated dancing turkeys.

Treatises have been written and theories formed on the origin of this strange freak of nature, but it still remains an unexplained phenomenon. Humboldt says (*Ansichten der Natur*,) that it is " an aggregating mass formed from a cosmical gaseous fluid." This is a very good thing to start with, but a scientific description would lead to awful language, with such an axiom as a leader—" oscillating," " upheaved," " fissured " are a few of the scientific plums one could bring in—but this is not a treatise.

We walked back tired and hungry, keeping

a bright look-out for snakes, with which the
place is infested. The coral snake, a beautiful
poisoner, and the boa-constrictor are all about
here, and I found the niggers knew of the fabled
amphisboena, the double-ender, and one of
the plank carriers had run away from one, very
ingeniously fleeing from him at right angles,
gaining time by puzzling his snakeship as to
which end to run at him with. I didn't quite
believe the nigger though. Plenty of alligators
reside in these pleasant regions too, and as we
traced our way back along the beach, our guide
pointed to tracks of this creature—but I knew
in my heart they were dog tracks!

On reaching the schooner we at once got
under way and beat up to San Fernando, the
second largest town of the island, situated near
a large and fertile plain covered with sugar
cane. It is apparently a central market for
parrots as every individual inhabitant has a
"polly" to sell—each supposed to possess super-
natural talent. The streets are quaint, tumble-
down houses like this, the homes of the centipede, and the gentle tarantula.

At San Fernando.

December 21*st.*—We received a very early visit from Mr. Bourne, the manager of the *usine* and sugar estates belonging to it at San Fernando. This, which is known as the Usine Centrale, is the largest in the West Indies, even larger than those at Martinique or Barbadoes, and grinds the sugar for all the surrounding estates, besides those belonging to it. It is, of course, owned by a joint stock company. We were very desirous of inspecting it, and although unfortunately the grinding season had not begun, Mr. Bourne came to conduct us over it, with planter's hospitality inviting us to breakfast at his charming house half-way between the town and the *usine*. After a very agreeable morning we visited the works, and from the passive boilers, flywheels, pumps and paraphernalia tried to gain an idea of the form and manner of making sugar, molasses and rum. I was more amused though, with the performance of a flourishing colony of ants, known as parasol ants, from the fact that each individual carries a leaf in his mouth which shades his back. These luxurious insects on being disturbed, rush into their holes and bring out a lot of very large chaps with big heads and tremendous nippers, who at once assume an attitude of self-defense, being in fact the bullies of the establishment; while the gentle parasol bearer stands aside to watch the fun. This is almost as surprising as Sir John Lubbock's statement that some tribes keep milch cows and also an old beetle whom they worship as an idol.

On our return to San Fernando we spent an hour or two at the hospital with the resident surgeon, and inspected some singular cases among the negroes, mostly caused by starvation or neglect. I saw among them a boy whose toes were almost destroyed by ulceration, caused by neglect of that insufferable pest, the *chigoe*. This almost microscopical little wretch burrows into the flesh and deposits a bag of eggs, which then have to be very carefully picked out with a needle, as breakage would ensure another batch. The niggers are very expert at this small surgery.

What with chigoes and ants, scorpions, centipedes, tarantulas and other tropical pests, I

Centipede.

would be quite willing to compromise on the mosquito. I extract the following from the *Edinburgh Review* to show that I at any rate don't exaggerate, and if it looks like it, Sydney Smith is to blame;

" The *tête rouge* lays the foundation of a tremendous ulcer. In a moment you are covered with ticks; flies get entry into your mouth, your nose; you eat flies, drink flies, and breathe flies; lizards, cockroaches and snakes get into your bed; ants eat up the books; scorpions

Scorpion.

sting you on the foot. Everything bites, stings or bruises: every second you are wounded by some piece of animal life. An insect with eleven legs is swimming in your teacup; a nondescript with nine wings is struggling in the small beer; or a caterpillar, with several dozen eyes in its belly, is straggling over the bread and butter. All nature is al've and seems to be gathering her entomological hosts to eat you up as you are standing, out of your coat, waistcoat and breeches!" *Rien que ça!*—

Tarantula.

We wound up the evening by an extremely jolly dinner at the house of the mayor, and a number of the male guests escorted us back to the schooner in the police boat, illuminated by the most superb moon I think even the tropics can exhibit.

December 22*d.* -We ran back to Port of Spain this morning and spent the day in most enjoyable silent rest. A dinner party in the evening took us ashore, and we were afforded a nice idea of the moral amusements of the nig-

gers, who are getting more noisy and obstrep-
erous as Christmas draws near.

December 23*d.*—The Prussian war brig "Undine" having run in here, we played a return
dinner match, and ended a peaceful day in a
very cheerful manner.

December 24*th.*—We went ashore soon after
daylight, to enjoy an excursion that had been
arranged for us to the Blue Basin, which lies
about twelve miles from Port of Spain in the
lovely valley of Marival. We started off on
horseback, and as soon as we cleared the Savanna met with a succession of delightful views,
all bounded by the mountains and the high
woods. Our road lay at first through well-cul-
tivated cacao plantations, with the industrious
coolies all at work, and occasionally a group of
the real Chinese, some of whom, by the bye,
own property and employ their Hindoo neigh-
bors; then over a high mountain; then down
into a valley, picking our way among boulders
and all manner of precipitous places, shaded
by great dark trees and the soft green of the

plantains, until we arrived at the Blue Basin, which, as its name indicates, is a very picturesque hollow scooped out of the mountain

John Chinaman.

side, and fed by a feathery waterfall coming down fifty feet from its stony furrow worn through the heart of the high woods.

4*

I wish I could fairly describe the luxuriance of lofty trees, and clinging, trailing, waving vines, creepers and parasites, all flowers and bloom—flowers, too, that look like huge butterflies and huge butterflies that look like flowers. The best description I know of is that by a true and devout lover of nature—Charles Kingsley.

We sat down to breakfast *al fresco,* surrounded on all sides by mountains clothed as I have tried to picture forth, but I previously took a " header " into the deliciously cold spring water of the basin and had a good swim, though it was disagreeable to dress while engaged in a vigorous dispute with a populous colony of ants, which had discovered my shirt and established aggressive outposts.

Our ride back was perhaps a little fatiguing, not to mention a certain loss of cuticle which impedes graceful motion, but this did not prevent us from going ashore at night to keep Christmas eve. As we rode through the streets at night to our friend's house, we were met by innumerable and pressing solicitations from the more than joyous coffee-colored population to assist them in a Merry Christmas. This season seems to remove all the mild restraints of civilization from the dark skinned races.

December 25th.—Christmas Day—we do not hear

"The clear church bells ring in the Christmas morn;"

but the niggers ashore have been making night hideous, with their howlings, fireworks and guns, worse than a bad attack of July 4th. And this morning they seem to be all drunk—men and women. We went ashore and found Mr. B—— waiting with his carriage to drive us out to the valley of Santa Cruz, about ten miles off, to visit Sir Joseph Needham who, besides being Chief Justice of the island, is a very successful planter of cacao, and his plantation adjoins that of Mr. B——.

Our drive led us through a more cultivated country than the visit to the Blue Basin, and we passed crowds of holiday keepers, negroes and coolies, the former mostly drunk, and the latter gorgeously attired after their picturesque fashion. Although the island belongs to the English, all the negroes speak the regular Martinique

French *patois*, and I envied Mr. B—— the facility with which he spoke the preposterous lingo.

Sir Joseph received us with planter's hospitality, and took a great deal of trouble to show us the method of drying and preparing the bean. He is reputed to be a most successful planter, and both he and Mr. B—— sell their entire crop to the eminent and advertising Epps.

We wandered around the shady plantation admiring the great gold pods, and the gorgeous *Bois immortelle*. But when we came to the *revocare gradum*, that was the labor and the work. Our amiable entertainer had involved himself in a labyrinth of trees and water courses, and we were lost on his own domain. It took a valuable half-hour to find our way back, for as we were to join a Christmas dinner party in town, we had to say "good-bye" and hurry off at once.

But "more haste, less speed" proved a true proverb on this occasion, for we "hadna ridden a league, a league, a league, but barely twa," when a hind spring of the carriage gave way, and we had to walk the horses into town, pre-

senting, ourselves, a ridiculously tilted appearance, with a weak tendency to slide down to ·
leeward. At last we were able to reach the
schooner, rush into our wedding garments, and
drive precipitately to the Savanna where our
amphitryon lived. Alas! we were an hour and
a half late. But though the repast had begun,
we made up for lost time and proved that the
end of a feast is better than the beginning of a
fray. What a Christmas dinner we had! fit
ending to our stay in this delightful isle, for we
leave to-morrow morning for Laguayra.

I find this singular entry in my journal:
" 2 A. M.—Alas! and woe isme! What shall
I do with G——'s plum pudding? *Miserere!*"

December 26th.—We waited all the morning
for the consul, who is to accompany us to Venezuela, to come off with the ship's papers and
so did not get under way till afternoon. At last
up goes the staysail, and away we go towards
the Bocas with a fair wind. Long lines of pelicans are flying along in shore, with the absurd
three flaps and a rest that distinguishes them,
and numbers of man-of-war birds are gliding

about so gracefully that one hardly sees the motion of a wing.

We soon reached the great ocean gates, and haul up on the wind into a most revolting sea. It seems quite a novelty to breast the great rollers, and pitch about once more, but is not quite so agreeable to our friend the consul, who falling into the clutches of old *Mal de Mer*, can only take safety in flight. He conquers him galantly, too, especially as we can soon lay our course with the wind more free. As night falls the weather becomes very squally, and our canvas is reduced to a minimum; it looks as if we were going to have one of the little "Josephine's" old-fashioned nights.

December 27th.—We *did* have an old-fashioned night if heavy squalls are worth mentioning, but fortunately they blew us on our way. The sea was very heavy, but in the morning it moderated, and we soon had all sail on her. First we sighted the Testigos, a group of rocky islands; then we coasted along Margarita island, thirty-eight miles long, with a very picturesque ridge of mountains about 5,000 feet high.

It is quite enchanting to cruise along right in the track of the old Genoese ; one does not wonder that he found everything so fair. His most admirable letters were written to their Catholic majesties, after his voyage over the course we are now visiting.

We had light winds in the middle of the day, but in the afternoon, a fine fair breeze set in, and we enjoyed a soft balmy air and a smooth sea.

December 28th.—We found that during the night the N. E. current had headed us off shore, so we had to change our course and stand in for the land, which soon rose above the horizon in mountains towering one above the other—beautiful, grand and picturesque. We got in with the shore about fourteen miles east of Laguayra, and as we run along with a fair wind and current under the shadow of this end of the immense Cordillera, extending the length of a mighty continent, I must quote from Washington Irving's life of Columbus, a description of the trip from Trinidad.

"Every day displayed some new feature of

beauty and sublimity; island after island where
the rocks, he was told, were veined with gold,
the groves teemed with spices, or the shores
abounded with pearls. Interminable ranges of
coast, promontory beyond promontory, stretching as far as the eye could reach; luxuriant
valleys sweeping away into a vast interior
whose distant mountains, he was told, concealed
still happier lands and realms of greater opu-
lence.

"When he looked upon all the region of
golden promise, it was with the glorious convic-
tion that his genius had called it into existence,
he regarded it with the triumphant eye of a
discoverer."

I don't think we can do anything of that
kind, but I know it is good to be here.
All that goes to make the character of a
landscape, the outlines of the mountains rising
one above the other into the vanishing distance,
the dark shade of the forests that clothe them,
the rushing torrents falling from overhanging cliffs, are so different from our northern
experiences, that we feel, indeed, in a new
world.

Columbus, whom I fear I am quoting rather too freely, supposed that he had reached an extension of the Asiatic continent when he first saw these beautiful shores. He believed that behind these mountains lay the apex of the world, reached by a gradual ascent as one penetrated the interior, and that the land would be found to increase in beauty and luxuriance until one arrived at the summit under the equator.

This he imagined to be the noblest and most perfect spot on earth, possessing a serene and heavenly temperature, with no deforming storms and tempests to mar its tranquility. In fact he believed this to be the original Garden of Eden—the terrestrial paradise—the original abode of our first parents!

All this and more, the poetical old discoverer wrote to his sovereigns of Castile, and one ardently sympathizes with his fancies on first breathing the pure delicious air and viewing the exquisite scenery of the coast we are now skirting.

At length we catch sight of a fort and citadel perched high upon the mountain, and at its base a straggly town stretching along the beach, which is Laguayra, the principal port of Venezuela. The port has no shelter, in fact it is not a port, but a bad open roadstead, and the anchorage is considered dangerous. We anchored, as it seemed, out at sea ; and certainly in a very heavy swell which broke in immense rollers on the beach. Heavens! how we did roll and pitch while waiting for the health officer and customs, and all the shipping anchored round us were curtseying and swaying in unison.

I have reason to believe, from the behavior of the officials after their inspection of the vessel, and from a conversation I chanced to overhear, that we were looked upon as very distinguished visitors indeed, and they actually sent a swell police boat to take us off. We had decided to sleep ashore, and start in the cool of the morning over the mountains to Caracas, the capital.

Landing is not so easy, however, as it seems at a distance, especially as there is no dock, but a little jetty, running out a short distance, with a flight of wooden steps at the end.

Our four rowers had to balance themselves near
the steps and ride over the rollers, till a comparatively smooth wave, when they rushed the
boat up to the steps, and we had to jump just
at the right moment. But, woe to the man who
doesn't know his own mind—an ounce of ir-
resolution obliges him to sit down again and
row off to wait another favorable chance.
Need I say that we all jumped the first time?

Deftly making our way through bales, boxes,
and laboring Indians and negroes, we were conducted through the quaint old Spanish town,
apparently full of churches and mules, to the
hotel, which stood in a narrow, hot street, all
front door and balcony. Hot! this is no expression for the sultry penetrating violence of the
sun's rays—which not only illuminate and burn,
but actually give color to objects.

Humboldt was right in saying that Laguayra
is the hottest town in the world. I think the hotel itself is the very quaintest object in the town
too, and looked so exactly like one of Doré's
illustrations to " Don Quixote," that I should
not have been astonished to receive an *œillade*
from Dulcinea del Toboso leaning over o. e of

the rickety wooden galleries, or to have seen Sancho Panza grooming Rosinante in a corner of the inn yard.

From our window we had a good view of the roadstead, and could see the gentle "Josephine," rolling away and turning up her bright copper at every surge. As soon as the heat diminished, we took a walk along the newly constructed Esplanade, a charming terrace above the ocean, but bordered on the land side by horrid-looking cabins and still horrider inhabitants, both unlovely and unvirtuous.

Returning to our quarters, we sat down to a supper-table, in company with several Don Quixotes and Sancho Panzas, in a sort of hall, open on one side; but the repast was too plentifully adorned with oil and garlic to be very palatable, and the butter was a singular composition of a deep orange color, and strange odor, resembling closely the beeswax and turpentine so dear to the house-cleaner. The chocolate was excellent, well prepared from the fresh bean itself—it deserves the name of *Theobroma*. Our beds were only a cot and a sheet, with no such superfluity as a mattress, consequently not so many fleas as I expected; but a certain scraping, wriggling and scamper-

A pleasant evening with a few friends.

ing, indicated that a varied assortment of domesticated animals were adding their tribute to the voices of the night. However, we are only to occupy them till four A.M., as that is the hour for our start over the mountains to Caracas.

December 29th.—I think we were none of us sorry to jump from our hard cots this morning, judging by the uncommon alacrity exhibited at so heathenish an hour. The early part of the night had been rendered hideous and intolerable by an unknown Frenchman in the room above us, who had done more in the way of varied noises with a pair of boots and a "scrooping" chair than belongs to mere mortals. Then C——had a cot which played a complicated tune every time he turned over, and he did so frequently. The most patient of us, at times, reviled his fate in terse language, whose echoes rolled from soul to soul, and kept one awake.

The watches of the night seemed interminable, although we were called at 4 A.M., before the casement had commenced to grow a glimmering square, and before 5 we were safely stowed in a coach, tho shabby picture of a *vettura*, harnessed with three horses abreast, " *buenos caballos Señores* "—which their looks belied sadly. The other sleepers in the hotel probably hailed our departure with curses as, with loud whip crackings, we rattled off over the narrow stony streets in the dark for two or three miles, before we turned off to breast the first spur of the mountain we had to ascend. The city of Caracas is, I believe, the site of the first mission founded by the Jesuits in this country, and those wise fathers planted it in a valley 3,500 feet above the sea level, so as to avoid the piratical and other ravagings that occasionally took place on the coast, one of which is splendidly described by Kingsley, in " Westward Ho." Hence, although only seven miles from Laguayra as the crow flies, to reach it we had to travel twenty-five miles, crossing the crest of the Pico de Nigantar, 5,500 feet high. We had crawled some distance up the zigzag ascent before dawn overtook us, and revealed a sight indescribably magnificent. During the whole ride we enjoyed a never-ending succession of exquisite views of lofty mountains, deep, wild, inaccessible ravines, and cloud-capped peaks, while from the heights and on the mountain sides immense cacti reared their bizarre forms against the sky, and innumerable aloes sent up their shafts of brilliant blossom. Standing in silent admiration of the scene, just glorified by the rising sun, one saw, far, far below

" The wrinkled sea beneath him crawl,"

forever breaking on the mighty continent whose
northern barrier we were scaling.

At the foot of the highest range we had to

The Mule Leader.

cross, we halted at a little *posada* or wayside
inn, a house of call for the mule drivers and
cartmen who line the road, night and day,

proceeding to or returning from Caracas. I counted over two hundred of them on the way, and then got tired of the amusement. Mules and donkeys under pack saddles or dragging carts, and loaded with the most heterogeneous collection of merchandise the imagination of man could evolve from his inner consciousness.

In the Procession.

The reason of this perpetual procession is that everything except sugar, coffee and cacao, and provisions, has to be hauled over the mountain

5

to the capital. Coal, for instance, sells there for $40 a ton, and all valuable things in proportion. We salute each mule-driver, in return to his grave " *Vaya con Dios*," unless he happens to have a cart, and then he is sure to be asleep in it, trusting to his sure-footed beast to avoid the precipices.

But all this while we are waiting in the *posada* for our refreshment, which consisted of boiled eggs, coffee, and a strange block of granite, which turned out to be particularly nasty cheese. The eggs, I imagine, were the production of some lean hens, gaining a precarious existence round the house, as on our clamoring for more (how hungry we were!) the very unamiable host said, "*No tengo mas;* " so, after paying a tremendous price for our entertainment, we *put on our overcoats*, so cold had it become, and topping the last steep peak, commenced descending towards the capital.

All along the road which, in its windings, is always open on one side to a sheer precipitous fall into the ravine—in fact, as remarked by Humboldt, it is very much like crossing the St. Gothard—I had noticed little piles of stones with a rude cross on the top. Now I understood that they marked the spot where a *coche* had tumbled over with its occupants. There are a good many crosses, and our burly conductor had a wooden leg, the result of a minor tumble.

It has been said, that in every individual lurks a vein of true genius. The golden thread in our driver was a capability of driving at full speed down the steep inclines, and so near to the unprotected edge as to cause the most sickly smiles to appear on all our faces, hiding the dread apprehension that after all, nothing would be left of us but a little pile of stones and a cross. Vehement expostulations produced a torrent of language most reassuring but quite incomprehensible to his victims.

We pass queer outlying huts of adobe, and land half enclosed by tumble-down mud walls. At last the path becomes smoother, more level, and by ten o'clock we rattle up to the barrier and halt to show our *pasaporta,* about which the authorities are very strict, as civil war is progressing in a very lively manner. The guard that turned out to receive us seemed good-looking soldierly men, but armed with guns and rifles of every variety and length.

The Guard House.

Passing the barrier we drove through quaint

narrow streets, catching glimpses of residences
sombre enough on the front, but with beautiful
interiors and with lovely gardens, through the
great Plaza, and at last pulled up at the hotel,
where we secured very nice apartments on the
Rez de Chaussée and looking into the street.
We were early enough to have a long time to
wait for the *table d'hôte*, breakfast, so a *siesta*
was declared at once—and I can sit down and
reflect that we have reached the capital of a
great South American republic. Venezuela
means "little Venice," and obtained this name
from Columbus, who first sailed into the great
gulf of Maracaibo, and discovered in its waters
and islands a fanciful resemblance to the Vene-
zia of his native land.

From the time that the South American col-
onies first shook off the yoke of Spain in 1812,
and disheartened by the terrible effects of the
earthquake, were again all but subdued, a long
and terrible struggle for independence ensued,
in which, if a parallel may be allowed, Bolivar
was the Washington, and José Paez the Putnam
of the battles, ambuscades, hair-breadth escapes,
and deeds of valor, which still form the topics

of conversation round the camp-fires of the
Llaneros. Paez was a special favorite with these
plucky fighters and hardy riders, and the song
has not been forgotten,

> " De todos los Generales cual es el valiente ?
> Mi General Paez con toda su gente !
> De todos los Generales cual es el mejor ?
> Es mi General José con su guardia de honor ! "

Under a rough form of provisional government, this determined people fought against
tremendous odds, patiently enduring all forms
of hardship and suffering till, in 1823, Puerto
Cabello was captured and Venezuela was pro-
claimed a free republic. It is natural to suppose that after such a long struggle the people
would have had enough of fighting, but in fact
the country has been more or less in hot water
up to a very late period, and revolutions and
rebellions have succeeded each other with short
interruptions. As soon as an officer attains a
a certain rank, if he can only reckon upon the
adherence of a respectable following of soldiers,
he begins to think of deposing the President
and stepping into his most uneasy shoes. It

has seemed as if they were actuated by avarice rather than ambition, as they usually levied large contributions and invariably pocketed the Custom Houses. Of course their rallying cries were always liberty or *libertad*, frequently two quite different ideas. I think *libertad* has never been a *principal* so much as a *dissatisfaction.*

Of a very different character is the President of to-day, Don Antonio Guzman Blanco. He is a man of noble qualities and lofty aspirations, and notwithstanding the fetters imposed on his actions by the prejudices and bigotry of parties, he has purified the government, pacified the country, and beautified the principal cities. A man of high education, and a natural statesman, he has been the first to surround the presidential office with stability and respect. It has not been without trouble though, and even while we were in Caracas he was in Barsiquimieto (a western state) with 14,000 men, giving the final blow to the last insurrection, which at one time was quite formidable, being fomented by the exasperated priesthood, whose religious houses Blanco had abolished and who brought much money and strong influences to bear against him. The neighboring island of Curaçoa was the headquarters of the " Blues," as the insurgents were called, and in that place were manufactured the surprising pieces of news which found their way into the newspapers of the United States. This great country of vast resources, producing sugar, cotton, coffee, cacao, indigo, tobacco and other spicy things in fertile profusion, is formed of twenty states, three territories and one federal district. Each state is ruled by a Governor, who is unwisely styled " President." The whole geographical area is 400,000 square miles, or about twice the size of France, while the population amounts only to 1,785,000 souls. The manner of taking the census, however, is necessarily imperfect, but the scantiness of the population can be traced to the political condition of the country, the constant struggle for *libertad*, and the terribly destructive earthquakes; banishment and epidemics, too, have done their share.

Under the present improved condition, the introduction of drainage to the cities, and the possibility of commercial as well as political tranquillity, the country must grow up to be a republic of the greatest commercial importance. Railroads are projected and other signs of approaching prosperity are not wanting, including a national coinage, which, when perfected, will I hope put a stop to the most dreadful confusion of *pesos sencillos, pesos Venezolanos, pesos fuertes* and all manner of inventions to bother and harass the weary traveller. As I make an end of recording these things, a welcome bell announces breakfast, and I must say that the hotel is the most perfect in its appointments and table that I have come across for a long time.

We were delighted with a repast where the *plats* were novelties, cooked with refinement, and which ending with a celestial cup of chocolate, enabled us to receive with fortitude the visits of a number of people brought by that indefatigable introducer, the consul. We strolled about the town, *flâned* round the shops, and found our way to the Plaza, a very pretty square planted with *palmas reales* and the "*flamboyant*," and adorned in the centre with a very artistic and beautiful bronze equestrian statue of Bolivar, presented to the country by the President Antonio Guzman Blanco.

The weather was simply delicious: the climate of Caracas has been justly called a perpetual spring. Standing as the city does on an elevated plateau surrounded by still higher mountains, it partakes of the tropic and temperate zones, and would produce wheat or peaches, but that the inhabitants seem to prefer planting coffee. The U. S. Minister, Judge Russell, took us out for a long drive in the afternoon, through a queer little Spanish village or two, past many coffee plantations, one of which we visited, passing up to the residence through beautiful grounds, when I again enjoyed the sight of wonderful orchids, recognizing particularly the splendid *Flor de l'Espiritu Santo* (*Peristeria elata*)—the flower representing a heavenly dove with outspread wings. We passed along the borders of the great fertile plains or *llanos*, which extend away through rich provinces, almost to the borders of Brazil, and of which I remember reading, with so much pleasure, Paez's " Wild Scenes in South America," all tales of adventure in these great plains, where the coffee harvest is now going on, although the other staple productions—tobacco, indigo, sugar, and cacao are of equal importance. The inhabitants of these *llanos*, or, as they are called, *llaneros*, are both riders and fighters, but with Hibernian indifference they will espouse any cause that will give them the arms they covet so much.

We returned by the road we came, always under the now deepening shadows of the Silla mountain, and skirting his buttress-like spurs. The mountain ascends abruptly from the plateau 8,500 feet—the first half covered with short grass, then a zone of evergreen trees, reflecting a purple light in the sunset, then crowning all, two bare rocky domes, which in temperate countries would be covered with snow. These domes and the hollow between them give the mountain its name (The Saddle).

The buttressed hills and spurs at its foot, reminded me of the method employed by Columbus to give Queen Isabella an idea of Jamaica; he crumpled a sheet of paper in his hand, and partly spreading it out, the hills, valleys, water-courses, etc., were well portrayed.

Humboldt's delightful account of his ascent of the Silla in 1801, to be found in his " Personal Narrative," gives one a sort of familiar interest in this mountain, whose great domes tower over the city into which we are returning.

In the evening, after an admirable dinner, we had an opportunity of seeing some of the lovely women for which the city is so justly celebrated.   Even the old Conquistadores tenderly related the beauty and grace of the savages they met with here, but *tantò*, the aborigines *quantò*, the goddesses of to-day, whose clear olive pallor, tender coffee-colored eyes, and lithe graceful forms, surpass all the traditions ; think then ! that they speak several languages, play classical music, wear Worth's dresses, and that in their hands the fan is a revealed language— and all ideas fall short of the dazzling reality ! —" ask me no more ! "

The men too, are handsome, and have beautiful, large, spaniel-like, sad eyes, and what Balzac calls " *cet air de tristesse dont les femmes sont*

si souvent les dupes." It was not quite safe
to be out late, though, for the half savage
soldiers who patrol the streets are quite prepared to shoot unless one can rapidly shout,
" *Patria y federales,*" which is the cumbrous
watchword the harmless citizen is expected to
be more than ready with. I shudder to think
what might might happen to a confirmed
stutterer.

December 30th.--What a night! Fleas!

Quis non flebit.

they came as the winds come when forests are

rended, " not in single spies, but in battalions ; " they feasted on us, they dwelt in our tents and they accompany us in our walks regardless of ammonia, which we have used in profusion, as well as camphor, with which I am drenched till I remind myself of a country funeral. I need hardly say that we got up very early, and walked out into the delicious morning air, and round the balconied streets, where I observed that the inhabitants build their houses as high as if there were no hereafter of earthquakes : they seem to take no lessons from the fearful past, and yet the market-place, some large convents and other buildings still stand in dilapidated, warning ruins. The only notice they take of their calamities, as I observed in our drive yesterday, in the suburbs particularly, is to place each house under the patronage of the Virgin, " *Impecado concebida,*" or a saint, and the names of these holy ones are painted in large letters on the front, as "*nostra Madre del Socorro, San Josef, San Vicénte de Paula, San Dimas* (the penitent thief) and lots of others. Some houses are copper-fastened with the names of two or three reliable ones all supposed to have these edifices under their particular care in case of a "*tremblado.*"

It is charming to read on the spot Humboldt's simple and beautiful narrative of the great earthquake of 1812, which laid the city in ruins and destroyed 20,000 people. In describing the universal terror that fell upon the inhabitants he says: "A number of marriages were contracted between persons who had neglected for many years to sanction their union by the sacerdotal benediction. Children found parents by whom they had never till then been acknowledged; restitutions were promised by persons who had never been accused of fraud; and families who had long been enemies were drawn together by the tie of one common calamity." So that it seems that even earthquakes have their appropriate moral and purifying influences.

We visited the churches this morning, and found services going on in them all, generally in one of the side chapels; the decorations are tawdry, and the pictures dauby; each chapel has its painted wooden saint, or ballet-dancing Virgin made up of dirty muslin, tinsel crown and spangles. The church of " *Merced* " still has its entire *façade* riddled with bullets and canister shot, quite unrepaired and left just as Guzman Blanco's troops defaced it, when he took Caracas in April, 1870. In the cathedral, we found a picture which, though in a shocking light and quite neglected, shone out like a moon among the dismal works of art beside it. It was a mother and child signed Velasquez in every brush-mark; although it is difficult to imagine how a picture of the heaven-taught court painter could have reached here.

High mass was being celebrated, very nasally intoned by a negro priest with a very white tonsure and a wall of black wool all around it, and a feeble organ accompanied his wobbly chanting. This instrument was supplemented in important passages by a tremendous trombone blown by another rather breathless nigger.

We strolled about the narrow streets till breakfast time, at short intervals going through the process of introduction to a part of the population. I had a set phrase concocted with great difficulty and a dictionary—" *Es muy triste que nosotros no hablar Español—Habla usted Francese?* This led to a rush of language " as when a river level with its dam," etc., to which it was only necessary to say "*mucho*" at intervals, and everything was lovely. Among others we met a colored gentleman, a near relative of the ace of spades, who was presented as General ——, with a whispered statement that he was high in command, and at the same moment a white beggar besought alms of him and us. This seems to do away with the old Spanish laconic : " *Todo blanco es caballero.*"

After breakfast and a *siesta*, L——, with the restlessness of the element he loves, and dreading the more introductions in store for us, began to collect the various documents and passports to enable us to leave. And in the afternoon, with a tender farewell to everybody, and an awful sum in equations before the hotel bill could be adjusted, we got into the corpulent carriage with the three horses and started back to Laguayra. Once more the exquisite scenery enchanted us, while the level rays of the setting sun were gilding clouds and peaks far below us. On the upper heights the

5*

evening silence was intense, and as we stopped
for a moment to enjoy the scene, I caught the
echo of the horns of Elfland faintly blowing from
cliff and scaur in the already shadowy distance.
It took us two hours less to return, as after the
highest peak is crossed, we had only to go full
speed down hill all the way. We got back to the
Don Quixote's hostelry by 7 o'clock, and after
more oil and garlick sought the society of our
fleas. I could not sleep—the memory of beautiful women, gorgeous scenery, Amyas Lee, the
Rose of Salterne, and some one at home lovelier
than she, ruined monasteries, the Inquisition—
all manner of incongruous thoughts stirred in
my busy brain, while through the casement came
the grand monotone of the sea, moaning out the
great settled sorrow at its mighty heart, the awful dream of the Deluge.

December 31*st.*—Cots, musical and otherwise,
also the ingenious French captain overhead,
were our portion last night, supplemented by
a visit from musquitoes. We spent the morning in a series of introductions—in offices and
in the street—to shopkeepers and strangers, to

officials, to an old colored woman, to a young ditto, to any and everybody that our guide, philosopher and friend chose to select. Our interviews were extremely flat, as our Spanish is very meagre.

We came across a number of emigrants from the United States who had been induced to come by the promise of high wages; the poor fellows could get no work, couldn't speak a word of the language, hadn't a cent among them, or any hope but that of getting to the mines, which is not a cheerful prospect. I believe they would have starved to death but for the humane exertions of Mr. Henry Kingan, the very admirable United States consul in Laguayra. He did us a very good turn too, for after waiting for hours to see the Spanish consul who was to endorse our bill of health, we at last discovered him in the shape of a very ugly brown little man with the dirtiest face I ever saw. He demanded such a tremendous fee for his endorsement, that we did not want it at that price, whereupon he tore our document in half, and danced about with rage. Mr. Kingan got us another one, while the little man was trying to have us arrested, and we got off to the schooner without molestation.

We soon hove up the anchor and hoisted the sails, and with a breeze that enabled us to defy a barrel of Spanish consuls, we departed from enchanting Venezuela, and as a farewell I will record a little story they tell in Caracas.

" You must know, then, that a few years ago Adam obtained permission to revisit the globe. He first alighted in Europe, and was quite lost, everything was so changed. His bewilderment continued until he reached Venezuela, then at last he clapped his hands: 'Ah! ah! here I am quite at home, this is exactly like the garden of Eden I was turned out of in such a hurry.' "

January 1*st,* 1875.—The happy new year sets in with a flat glary calm. We are only about twenty miles from the coast, and the mountains loom dark on the brassy hot horizon. The schooner curtseys lazily to the long oily swell that reflects back every rope and spar, and plenty of great crafty-eyed sharks glide round about us, occasionally floating up to the surface. One of them about as long as the gig, has such a strange resemblance to an eminent Massachusetts lawyer and politician, that we determine if possible to capture him ; but, like his great prototype, he is too wary to take any notice of our bait, perhaps we ought to have trolled with a spoon !

In the afternoon, a pleasant breeze springs up, and nightfall finds us making good way towards San Domingo, our next objective point. We have been compelled to abandon our visit to Jamaica, as the small-pox is raging there, and quarantine is abhorrent to our souls.

January 2d. — Tearing into a heavy sea, reefed down fore and aft, we had a day in all respects the opposite of yesterday. We are rolling and waltzing about, and the water flies over us right merrily.

Soon after noon, we decide to omit San Domingo from our cruise, rather than be as uncomfortable as we are likely to be close-hauled across a strong current ; and as we head round for Santiago de Cuba, we bring the wind abeam and case the craft a good deal, notwithstanding a very heavy beam sea; but then a quiet night is a *desideratum* always.

January 3d.—Our modest desires were not granted last night, for we had heavy squalls in both watches, and for the first time since leaving the North Atlantic, our old stand-by, the main trysail, reappeared, vice mainsail furled; but this morning the breeze has settled into a steady blow, so we turn out the reefs, set the mainsail, and bowl off ten knots handsomely.

To-day is a capital specimen of sailing in the Caribbean sea; exquisite blue water, and blue sky, with here and there a fleecy cloud; our swelling sails bending to the breeeze, and our gentle "Josephine" leaning over to it, curtseying her way along, scaring the flying-fish, which jump out and scurry away in shoals almost every yard we go. I don't believe, though, that they are all frightened. Sometimes one or two, sometimes a hundred, will get up like a bevy of quail, and whirr off, just tapping the crest of a wave for a wet, and I have seen them make

a good three hundred yards before dropping.
They can change their flight, and turn off at
right angles like a swallow. At night, attract-

Flying-fish.

ed by the lights, they fly on board, and one
hears them come flop! against a sail, and drop
on deck. The sailors are very fond of them,
and they are not wasted.

In the afternoon our old squalls set in again,
and we double reef down, but average nine
knots all the same, in a heavy sea.

January 4th.—We are now sailing along the southern coast of San Domingo, but about fifty miles from it. And the heavy sea that breaks over us occasionally, is said to be a *specialité* of this coast. The squalls gradually settle into a strong breeze, and the schooner walks away with it like a witch.

January 5th.—Running before it, we had a quiet night, under double reefed mainsail and staysail. At midnight we hauled up to run into the Windward passage, between Hayti and Jamaica, and at daylight the lofty blue mountains of Cape Tiburon were in sight about fifteen miles off at our starboard hand. The sun rose gloriously over them, and seemed to have mixed a new color, from the pigments on the solar palette, a rich cream color, quite indescribable.

The day has been the most completely perfect one that we have had since our cruise began. An exquisite cloudless sky—just a mere ripple on the ultramarine of the sea, and a soft balmy air, not uncomfortably hot—just a day to tempt the beautiful purple " Portuguese man-of-war " or *nautilus* on a cruise, and we see numbers of them floating by with their tiny sails set, and their fleshy-looking ballast properly disposed of underneath them.

Towards sunset we catch the first glimpse of the distant mountains of Cuba's southern coast in a purple haze. "Whilst glow the heavens with the last steps of day" we speak a barque, the "Greenville Belle," of Annapolis, N. B. She looked gigantic in the level light, with every sail set reflecting back "the rosy depths." We hung together for a moment, and then, with shouted farewells and dipping of colors, went our own ways *Quà cursum ventus!* Who could help thinking of dear old Arthur Clough's sweet verses?

> "As ships becalmed at eve, that lay
> With canvas drooping, side by side,
> Two towers of sail, at dawn of day
> Are scarce long leagues apart descried.

> "When fell the night, up sprung the breeze,
> And all the darkling hours they plied;
> Nor dreamt but each the self-same seas
> By each was cleaving, side by side.

> "E'en so—but why the tale reveal
> Of those whom, year by year unchanged,
> Brief absence joined anew, to feel
> Astounded, soul from soul estranged?

" At dead of night, their sails were filled,
And onward each rejoicing steered;
Ah ! neither blame, for neither willed
Or wist what first with dawn appeared.

" To veer, how vain ! on, onward strain,
Brave barks ! in light, in darkness too !
Through winds and tides one compass guides—
To that and your own selves be true.

" But O, blithe breeze ! and O, great seas !
Though ne'er, that earliest parting past,
On your wide plain they join again,
Together lead them home at last.

"One port, one thought, alike they sought—
One purpose hold, where'er they fare ;
O bounding breeze, O rushing seas,
At last, at last, unite them there !"

January 6th.—We ran in so close to the land that L—— thought best to heave-to about midnight. C—— and I, overwrought by the brilliant stars (how much nearer they seem to us than they do at home), had been singing songs that we had heard girls sing at Newport, until we drifted into complete spooneyness, and turned in with the vague woe of uncertainty that haunts a man who has had no news of home or kindred for nearly three

months. This has been our fate owing to the
preposterous mail system of the West Indies.

This morning at dawn we found ourselves
well under the land about fifteen miles from the
Morro Castle, and had to endure a season of
calm before the sea breeze at last came to cool
us and gently waft us to our haven. The Cobre
mountains which form the southern coast barrier, do not seem so imposing after those of
Venezuela, and are very bare and scant of vege-
tation. The Morro Castle and lighthouse glit-
tered on the heights a good way off, and it was
afternoon before we reached the little narrow
opening that leads up to Santiago de Cuba. Not
more than a cable's length across, the little strait
looked like a cleft in the rocks, and perched
over it was the Morro Castle, a queer old-time
fortification, something like Chillon, with a bit
of the tower of London stuck into it, red,
weather-stained, moss-grown, picturesque, the
very emblem of Old Spain and its crumbled
chivalry, its old traditions and glories, and its
catholic hatred of innovation. "That a fort!"
said C——, "why, a single poor little iron
clad could knock its beautiful old battlemented

walls and pignons into a cocked hat in half an hour." And so it could. But what a shame it would be ; nothing could ever replace the quaint old-world tumble-down representative of the nation it belongs to, and it would be as great a crime whitewashing Westminster Abbey. (*Sic parva componere cum magnis solebam.*)

We took on board a Chinese pilot, whose language was an utterly unintelligible polyglot, and after responding to interrogatories from the fort, hurled at us through an enraged speaking-trumpet, we passed close under the wave-worn cliff, noticing at its base a large dark cave full of bats and birds, darting about in the gloom. With many twistings and windings we slowly sailed up the narrow river——whose banks, but for the many aloes, with their lofty shafts full of blossoms that glorified them, reminded us of the Hudson River, just below West Point—until the city of Santiago appeared in sight.

We glided on until the pilot had got us between two men-of-war, (one of which was the "Tornado," the capturer of the "Virginius"), and not till we were thoroughly under their guns did we let the anchor go, with the crashing froth, and chinking run and jolt of the chain-cable, that is so pleasant to hear after some days at sea.

We were at once boarded by the health officer and custom-house people, with their "tail" of interpreters and assistants. These gentry, very much like their fraternity in Aguadilla, could not understand the object of a yacht, the "Josephine" being, according to them, the first *goëleta de récreo*, ever seen in these waters. These officials were quite uncomfortable, but "a soft answer turneth away wrath," and L——'s dignified explanations, especially as they didn't understand half of them, had a soothing influence, so that they partook freely of sherry, and left us with only the parting legacy of a custom-house watchman, his blanket, and his ordinary supply of fleas. He squints dreadfully, and his color varies like a chameleon's, but he seems harmless. They are not so bad as the Aguadilleros though, for we are not quarantined, and we have permission to go ashore.

Whilst we were dining the captain of the

port came off, a very charming fellow indeed
He withdrew the squinter at once, and brought
invitations to a grand ball at the Club, given in
honor of the young King Alfonso, of which
we are now first made aware. To-day is, besides, the *Dio del Reis* or Twelfth-night, a
very grand holiday among the negroes, especially among those who are slaves, and we were
made aware of it at sundown by a battery near
us opening fire with a royal salute.

We landed, accompanied by our new-made
friend the captain, and first walked up to the
Plaza de Armas to hear the bands play. It was
one of the prettiest sights imaginable. The
Plaza was half illuminated by lamps hung in
the trees; it was full of people, and the walks
were lined with ladies sitting down or walking
round the square; most of them were going
to the ball, and their dresses were very handsome. I never saw so many very pretty women together, except in a ball room in New
York (which goes without saying).

Their hair seems as glossy as a blackbird's
wing, and their fans wave and languish in that
enchanting manner proverbial with the Donna

of Spain, and their feet—ah! I have seen few feet even, in New York, like those, though they cannot erase the memory of a mite whose unsurpassable little feet have trampled on my heart these years past; but it is not only that their feet are so small or so *bien chaussés*, it is the *démarche.* These ladies do not walk, they float; they pass like Junos in a gliding, Olympian motion, unaccounted for by any mechanical laws.

I was presented to a number of charming people, who all spoke French more or less; but it was a deuce of a task to remember their names —and when they dropped into their own soft Cuban Spanish I could only stammer and look like a goose. We stayed till the ball was well under way, and tired to death we went on board, just looking in for a few moments at the ball, which appeared to be taking place in the Club, in the street and all round the neighborhood— and it was funny to see beautifully dressed young women with bare heads and necks, standing in the street and peering through the blinds at the dancers.

The U. S. consul is absent, but his Vice, who

is a very clever and amiable fellow, has already taken a great deal of trouble for us. He did not, however, introduce us to more than thirty or forty people to-day, which is by no means an abuse of his opportunities.

January 7th.—We landed this morning to pay a visit of ceremony to the Governor of the District, General Marin, who lives in a very swell palace on the Plaza. He looks a good deal like Louis Napoleon, only more so. He received us very politely, and cigars were handed round, just like coffee and chibouques in the East. As he spoke French admirably, we were quite *en pays de connaissance,* but just as we took leave of him, he sprung a most unpleasant little mine on us, by suggesting that we were liable to a fine of five hundred gold dollars for not having a "*manifiesto.*" Here was a "go" —the dreadful spectre of Aguadilla confronted us once again—again the Treasury department's commission was waved in the air similar unto the "Stars and Stripes," and oh Lord! a certain *superior smile,* the patent for which I thought belonged exclusively to two persons in New

York, appeared on the General's handsome face. I admit that I cowered—the superior smile had completely done for me; but our skipper rose to the occasion, and we retreated in good order.

Evidently we were to have all over again the roaring farce of Aguadilla—exactly repeated, indeed, as the first act ends by *Tableau* I. The wicked collector has a dream of five hundred gold dollars. *Tableau* II. The authorities send a telegram to the Captain-General in Havana for instructions.

On leaving the Governor we presented a letter of introduction to Mr. B——, who is the chief merchant here, and the advice and assistance of himself and his partners have been both soothing and agreeable. There is no doubt, however, that the Porto Rico dénouement will end the little comedy.

The city of Santiago is built on a spur of the Cobre mountains, and rises in an amphitheatre from the harbor, which is completely circular, large, and lies like a basin between the two mountains. Like all the Spanish towns we have seen, the streets are narrow, sordid and undrained, and most of them are provided with

6

dreadful stinks of their own, which gives the liberal allowance of five fearful smells to the acre. Coleridge's description of Cologne is but a faint outline of the capacity of Santiago in this particular.

A large transport steamer arrived this morning from Cadiz, and anchored near us. She was crowded with a thousand unfortunate Gaditani recruits for the army. They are all mere lads, and too good-looking—when one sadly thinks how many of them will be *gastados* by disease and neglect before six months are over their heads. The Spaniards have not a good record here for taking care of their sick wounded.

The headquarters of the *mambis* or (insurgents) are not more than three leagues or so from the city, in the mountains, but it is very difficult to get any information about them, or even to get people to talk about them at all. They are either flourishing and always advancing with decided success, or else they are a handful of bandits on their last legs, according to the sentiments of the speaker, or the office he holds under the crown.

Introductions and interviews have done their work, and not even the prospect of music in the Plaza can attract us from the cool, quiet deck of the schooner.

January 8th.—We had a long quiet morning on board, with a few visitors. We wished very much to pay a votive visit to the slaughter-house abreast of which we were anchored, the appropriate scene of the butchery of the wretched prisoners from the "Virginius." But the consul dissuaded us, on the score that it might give umbrage to the authorities, who must be very sore on the subject of Americans. So we went ashore to the Club *de San Carlos*, a very handsome building on the Plaza, where we went through the usual course of introductions. The club rules here are more elastic than those which obtain at home, for on music nights at the Plaza, after the band has played through its programme, the members capture it and convey it to the club where, having invited the ladies of their acquaintance they find upon the Plaza, they have a dance and a regular lark. It is an idea to be followed.

Underneath all this gaiety on the surface, however, is concealed a great deal of misery, many good families being reduced completely to want by the loss of their plantations, or by the enormous taxes imposed upon capital and income both, (*five per cent.* on the former, and *ten per cent.* on the latter,) besides other exactions which sometimes I fear take the form of forced loans, in reality forced robberies, for the government pays no one. Even the troops have been unpaid for many months, yet the repinings are as yet only feebly whispered or left unuttered.

We learn that the Captain-General has sent a telegram with instructions to place the "Josephine" on the same footing as an English yacht in Spanish waters. This ends the *comedietta*, which nevertheless gave us some uneasy moments.

After walking through the city a few times, although it is the ancient capital of the island, there is nothing to attract one ashore, and the smells are so repulsive that one can hardly stand it. There is a new one at the corner of every street lying in wait to knock you down. There are plenty of pretty faces, to be sure ; but then it is " only a face at the window " and nothing more.

The streets are in a wretched condition, as the money extorted from the inhabitants all goes to

Family Provisions.

Spain, and none of it is spent upon the city. The colored population feed chiefly on sugar-cane if one may judge by their dilapidated front teeth, and groups like these which are constant-ly to be seen in the streets. I went into a pleasant galleried, clean-looking hotel kept by

a stout old colored auntie known as Madame
Adelé, who had been a Martinique slave in her

Sweet Content.

youth.   She became quite chatty over the misfortunes of Cuba.   "*C'est un pays tout à fait
vêdu, pêdu, pêdu, oui monsieur, pêdu!*" she
said, reminding me of *La Fille de Madame An-
got*, as she turned away to scold some coffee-colored young women in the same delectable *patois*.

On our way back we encountered a large
funeral train of *volantes*, drawn by very handsome mules, accompanied by a long tail of
slaves who seemed to consider it rather a game.

It was the funeral of a young girl, and the

coffin was borne into the church covered with beauteous flowers, which were strewn round in profusion. It made me think of Chateaubriand's " Elise : "

> " Ah ! ne les rends jamais à ce monde profane,
> A ce monde—rempli d'angoisses et de douleur,
> Le vent brise et flétrit, le soleil brûle et fane
> Jeune fille et jeune fleur.

> " Tu dors, pauvre Elise si légère d'années
> Tu ne sens plus du jour ni le poids ni la chaleur
> Elles ont achevé es leurs fraîches matinées
> Jeune fille et jeune fleur ! "

The service was very fine, but all solemnity was destroyed by the dulcet tones of fiddle and horn which were employed to fortify the organ, especially as immediately after the service we met the big fiddle scurrying out in the arms of its ebony performer.

We stayed on board after dinner and discussed spiritualism in our shirt sleeves—*musquitoes.*

January 9th.—We went ashore to *flâner* at the club, but after once seeing the quaint old town, there is nothing to interest one, and it is sad to see the abandoned houses, the decayed families and homes, caused by the insurrection and its results. The ruin is sure, and although slower than an earthquake's ravages, is less merciful. The Spanish part of the population merely shake their heads, but are unwilling to speak of it in any way.

January 10*th.*—We went to the cathedral this morning and heard the celebration of High Mass; the organ was excellent, but the singing nasal and below mediocrity. The aisle was filled with pretty women in long rows, each with her private rug to kneel upon, and the men sauntered about between the pillars, casting tender glances at the kneeling objects of their devotion. As soon as Mass was over the band struck up in the Plaza, and the fair worshippers paraded about to be worshipped in turn. But there was no display of costume, as it seems to be *de rigueur* for the ladies in church to wear black with a very becoming black vail.

In the afternoon we got a couple of *volantes*, and guided by the consul visited an *estan-*

cia (which is a sort of large garden-farm) belonging to M. Ducourcau, a Frenchman, who
has just received summary notice to leave the
sland within twenty-four hours. His banish-
nent, which is quite arbitrary, without trial of
any kind, is not easy to understand unless it be
his intimacy with the U. S. consul, as the only
reason given by the authorities for his banishment is " intimacy with the enemies of Spain."

The *estancia* is a very pretty place with exquisite gardens, a large dwelling, fountains,
baths, etc., but all with a sort of *lezardé* half
ruined air, fitting the misfortunes of its owner,
who seemed a bright, polite, intelligent little
man, with nothing of the conspirator about him
unless it was a " *collet noir.*" His farewell to
his bereaved family took place while we were
there, much to our confusion, but it did not seem
to be an overwhelming separation—indeed our
attention was at once turned to a tarantula of
about the circumference of a soup-plate, whose
hairy life I ruthlessly took—and the departure
of the " banished lord," in a *volante*, surrounded
with his trunks, excited scarcely a ripple.

We soon took our leave and drove about four

miles further to a village called Caney, where
they were having Sunday high-jinks in celebration of the proclamation of the young king.
The sports consisted of a greasy pole, of course
so greasy that none of the little bronze statues
swarming at its foot could get very high, and
the atmosphere was full of cries of what I should
take to be the Spanish for "boost me, Billy."
There was a goose, too, tied by the legs in the
centre of a rope, and the thing to do was, being
blindfolded, to knock the wretched bird's head
off with a club—in fact the fair was full of
sprees dating from the cruelties of the barbar-
ous Dark Ages.

We wandered round the village, half deserted and half in ruins, surrounding a little church
embedded in brick fortifications, built round it
like red-bath tubs; for the *mambis* or insurgents, who are hiding about on the other side
of the mountain, are always threatening it. As
we returned along the road, which is never repaired, and in the most break-neck disorder, we
we couldn't help noticing the hopeless look of
the old plantations, and once lovely *estancias*,
all grown over and full of weeds running riot,

and this within five miles of the second city and the old capital of the island.

We were glad to hasten *home*—for association and long occupation makes a home of the dear old " Josephine "—to enjoy the cool freshness of the harbor.

January 11th.—Our excursions outside the city being quite limited, by the advice of the residents, on account of the proximity of the *mambis* who appear to behave to everybody like the beggar in *Gil Blas*, we decided to depart to day, and early in the afternoon our pilot came aboard. Once more we hoisted sail to a nice breeze and ran merrily out of the harbor, but close to the Morro the wind entirely deserted us, and we had nothing to do but to anchor and wait for the *terral* or land breeze, which is very uncertain in its visits. The waters about here and the town itself recall vividly that charming book " Tom Cringle's Log," having been the scene of many of the adventures and descriptions it contains, and we certainly were anchored in a most piratical looking place, full of little nooks and corners for a small vessel to

hide away in. We met in Santiago a gentleman named Mr. Thomas Bell, who is the grand-
son of the *Don Ricardo Campañero* of Tom
Cringle, and who had returned to the original
Scotch appellation.

The land breeze cometh not, and we turn in
in perfect quiet, although out beyond we can
see the white surf dashing up on the cliffs.

January 12*th.*—At dawn we slipped out
from the cool gray shadows of the land into a
smooth sea and a favoring breeze, which latter,
however, soon dwindled to a faint breath, so
that all day long we just fanned along the shore
very slowly, opening point after point of the
Cobre mountains. Although well wooded
they are more pretty than picturesque; but
perhaps we have seen so many fine "*paysages
accidentés*" that our eyes are fatigued as one's
are after doing a room or two at the *Louvre.*

It does not require much imagination to-night,
looking over the hills with the soft moonlight
silvering their outlines, to convert a fire we
observed in one of the darker valleys, into a
wild *mambi* camp and bivouac, as we know

that they are hidden somewhere in the vicinity.

Towards midnight a large war steamer passed about a mile from us, close into the land, and we expected fully to be brought-to and overhauled; but she made no sign as she glided past us, and left us to turn in, in peace.

January 13th.—"All night no ruder airs perplex her sliding keel," but a very light breeze brought us at dawn abreast of Mount Turquino, a noble mountain rising 8,400 feet, and an important landmark.

Throughout the day we loitered along till we passed Cape Cruz in the afternoon, and stretched away towards Cape Antonio, 450 miles distant, which we must round to reach Havana, our next port.

At night we had a sudden and violent squall, which brought in our kites pretty quickly, and when it subsided, left us with a pleasant breeze; a very agreeable change from the sultry sauntering of the last two days. It was very pleasant, too, to see a cloud in the perfectly uniform blue arch overhead. They have been so rare lately that the sudden shadow of one over the dark unfathomable blue water, falls dramatically, like an event.

January 14*th.*—Out of sight of land—pleasant breeze—smooth sea—complete and happy repose.

January 15*th.*—Just the same as yesterday—both days being the perfection of sailing weather; we are nearing the land, and are looking out for the light on the cape.

January 16*th.*—At three A. M. we sighted the light on Cape San Antonio, and thence passed through the strait between that point and the main land of Yucatan, out into the Gulf of Mexico, having still 180 miles to beat to windward against the trades, before we can make Havana—a somewhat disagreeable prospect after such delightful smooth and dry sailing.

January 17*th.*—All day we have been making long tacks, occasionally catching a shadowy glimpse of the land, and we hope to reach our destination to-morrow.

January 18*th.*—We sighted the Morro Castle at daylight, but beating against a light wind were unable to pass that splendid old fortress until afternoon, when we anchored amidst a fleet composed of shipping of all nations.

The beautiful rock-bound entrance to this port is familiar to almost every one, but one can never approach it without renewed admiration, and a remembrance of all the old legends and stories of pirates and buccaneers, of bloody battles and cutting-out slavers, that in the readings of one's childhood were connected with " The Havannah." Even Burns has written :—

> " I served out my trade
> Where the bloody game was played,
> And the Morro low was laid
> At the sound of the drum ! "

As we lower our sails and shoot up to our anchorage in the upper part of the harbor, I am astonished at the great apparent increase to the trade of the place since I was here in 1861, as shown by the shipping crowded together all around us.

On landing I find that the same great change has been effected in the old town. The ancient fortifications have almost disappeared, and "extra Muros" has lost its signification; the beautiful old private dwellings, in the chief streets, are converted into stores, thus effacing the fourteenth century. And even the Plaza de Armas, where the band used to play the *Rétreta* every night, is very shabby, and the four royal palms round the monument in the centre, look droopy and ashamed of their humbled condition. As for the Dominica, the swell *café* of old, it has sunk to a shabby old coffee-house, lurked in by men with blue chins, who consume greasy pastry and repel the assaults of ragged venders of lottery tickets. Volantes, too, have disappeared, except at funerals, though what their particular appropriateness to that ceremony consists of is past finding out, to any one who remembers their ancient splendors; their places are filled by herds of nasty little victorias, which are wonderful lurking places for the most vicious fleas. All the gaiety, clubs, and wealthy people have moved beyond the old walls, where a large city has

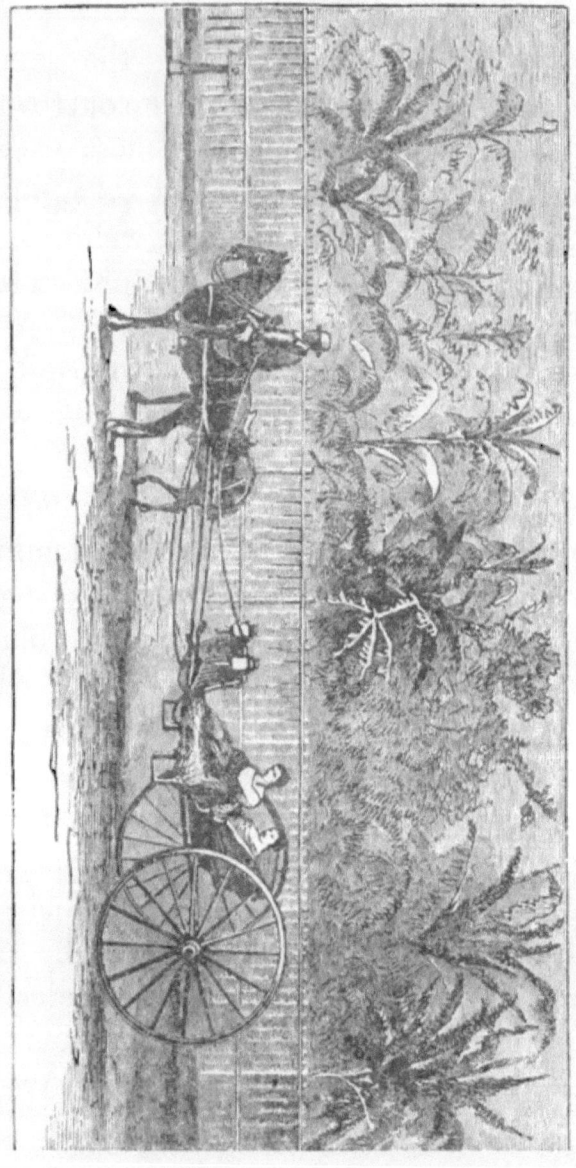

Havana—The Cuban Volante.

sprung up, with handsome wide streets, squares, etc., almost European in appearance.

Here, at last, we find all our letters from home, accumulated from different ports where they missed us. It is a delightful thing to open, one after another, the filmy envelopes, and while re-assured of the well being of one's own Penates, to exchange the scraps of *chronique scandaleuse* with the other letter-readers, who both, I observed, opened their last-dated letter first, as indeed I did too. Think of three months' scandal and gossip all at once! Add to this all the magazines and new novels, well selected by Brentano, and devise a pleasanter afternoon for three wanderers, if you can.

Thank goodness! the one crumpled rose leaf is gone that made my couch uneasy. Of course, in the long dearth of news all manner of misgivings assailed me, especially in those sad wakeful small hours of the darkness "when my light is low." Now they are exorcised and gone.

There are a number of Spanish men-of-war in the harbor, among others the "Arapiles," whose infelicitous experiences in New York may be still remembered. She has just mounted a gorgeous gold crown over her figure-head, in honor of the new *régime*. Indeed, it is surprising the rapidity with which, down to the merest tub of a gun-boat, they have all replaced the crown in the national colors, which had disappeared with the Bourbon.

What with the heavily armed Morro Castle and the fortress of the Cabanas on the one side, the powerful fort at the Punta on the other, and the many war ships round us, it looks as if the Spaniards had taken every precaution against losing possession. Here, however, we had no sort of trouble in getting settled. The customhouse visit was a polite form, and at last they understood the possibility of a *goëleta de recréo*, although the boatmen who ply about the harbor will insist on calling the dear little schooner "*El Pilot Bote Americano*," to L——'s intense disgust.

January 19*th.*—If any man having partaken of the many larks of Havana, till the "wee sma' hours," wishes to borrow a few hours' rest from the day, let him not hope for it within earshot

of the harbor, for at five A. M., long before
dawn, the flag-ship "Arapiles" fires off a tremendous gun which, as we are lying alongside of
her, shakes us from stem to stern. Then to
prevent our going to sleep again, from every
other man-of-war in the place, one or more
trumpeters, the tootelary guardians of the port,
commence a fearful brazen howling which lasts
till long after sunrise. I think it must be intended to strike terror into the hearts of the
Englishmen on a pretty corvette called the
"Eclipse," which ran in here yesterday from
Jamaica, and gave rise to a vast deal of noisy
saluting.

We took a drive on the *Paseo*, but it was not
a very gay one. The insurrection seems to have
destroyed all the fashionable life of the place.
The old race of Spanish residents who made the
glories and the gaieties for which the city is
so renowned, are gone, either ruined or retired
to Spain, and their places are filled by a new
and totally different class, who are not residents
but sojourners, to make money as fast as possible and leave. I believe that the Spanish
population even, in their hearts look upon the

island as *lost to Spain.* It seems now to be only a question of time and holding out. The *mambis* have been at it since 1868, and although they never venture their fortunes in a pitched battle, they are always on the alert, harassing the columns of the troops sent against them, and kill a fearful number of them, almost in security, from their knowledge of the forests and mountain passes, which precludes the possibility of active or effectual pursuit. Then the Emperor of Russia's old brutal boast of his two greatest generals, *Janvier* and *Février*, is quite paralleled here, for disease and exposure decimate the poor unacclimated boys, who compose the Spanish rank and file.

The prices of everything are very high, and they seem enormous at first, but as they are given in "*papel*," of which a good deal can be got for a very little gold, it is not so bad as it seems.

January 20th.—Ashore all day, making one visit and another, in the midst of tremendous preparations that are being made on all sides for a grand "*fiesta*," to last three days, in honor

of the coronation (this time) of King Alfonso.
To-morrow is the first day of the trouble, and

Street Scene in Havana.

strings of mules pervade the street, laden with

all manner of green stuff to decorate doorways; the mules are completely invisible, so that they look like a procession of the whole of Birnam's woods.

In the evening we went to a ball at Mrs. Almy's hotel, near the Punta. It was a very jolly dance, with plenty of old friends there, and I had a pleasant remembrance and greeting from the hostess, who was just as nice as ever, and went about the room looking like a dear old smiling wax-work in gold spectacles. We looked in, too, at the Casino club opposite the Tacon theatre, the most gorgeous concern I ever saw, as to size and gilding. It is a political institution, and the head-quarters of the Spanish or anti-home rule party. Zulueta, the chief slave owner of the island, is the President of it, and all the volunteers and city tradesmen are fierce members.

Notwithstanding a very jolly day, I do feel that Havana is greatly changed for the worse, and everybody seems to go about deploring the sad fact.

January 21st.—Again does the great gun

shake us from our slumbers, and the beastly bugler " pours through the mellow horn his pensive soul." Yet, after all, Havana is a very jolly place indeed, when you get extra muros; especially is it nice to saunter about the large sort of a Champs Elysées that lies in front of the Tacon, and observe the manners and customs of the *Señors*, not to mention the *Señoras* and *Itás*.

While pottering about the streets this morning, visiting and shopping, we strolled into the Cathedral, and an obliging little Melchisedec, with a big tonsure, bore us up to the chancel to see the tomb and monument of Christopher Columbus. So after following in his steps and enjoying his discoveries, we stand before his last resting-place,

"Two handfuls of white dust shut in an urn of brass,"

in the island that he discovered, and where he first planted the standard of the Cross.

The monument, however, is only an insignificant mural tablet in the hideous taste of the early part of this century, and the nose is damaged besides, while the glorious old mariner's bones appear to be stuffed into a sort of safe let into the wall. But it is a curious instance of " Time's revenges " that his mortal remains should have been transferred from San Domingo, and deposited with reverential pomp in the very place where, three hundred years before, he had been cast into prison and loaded with chains!

In the evening we had an invitation from the Captain-General (to whom we had presented a letter of introduction), to a reception at the Quinta de los Molinos, his country-house on the Paséo. We found a lot of men, mostly in uniform, sitting on a splendid large marble piazza, smoking, chatting, and listening to the music of an admirable band stationed among the trees. Both the house and grounds are remarkable for their beauty and the order in which they are kept. General Concha received us very civilly, and fortunately for us spoke French very well. The dignity of our arrival was, perhaps, marred by the fact that, worse than Rawdon Crawley, we actually did enter the presence of the " sovereign " in a hack-cab, which was of the worst and most flea-haunted description; and as a climax, the wretched brute that drew it, after many stumblings, broke down right in front of the brilliant assemblage, and mildly but firmly declined to get up again, or do anything but twiddle his ears in a hopeless manner.

General Concha, who is a well preserved man about sixty, has that sort of family look of Louis Napoleon that I have seen so often in Cuba—he had a red silk belt round his stomach as a distinguishing mark. I congratulated him on the accession of the young Bourbon, but I don't think he really cared two pence about it.

That Champs Elysées place is really delightful by moonlight!

January 22d.—Is but a chronicle of gastronomy. We had breakfast on the "City of New York," one of the fine steamers of the Alexandre line, and I only wish some of the transatlantic lines would study their *ménu.*

In the evening we dined with the British vice-consul (Mr. Crawford), who lives in a great rambling creole kind of edifice, very cool and comfortable, a long way up the Cerro, and from the boat landing until we reached his

house, we drove under one long arcade of san-
guinary looking bunting; the fronts of the
houses and shops were all festooned too, with
the gaudy national colors.

There was a grand display of fireworks at
1 ight, but who would desert a pleasant dinner
to see fireworks? and so ended the first *dia de
festa.*

January 23d.—We were aroused from our
peaceful slumbers this morning by a fearful
cannonading from the men-of-war in the
harbor, which proved to be a most untimely
salute of twenty-one guns from every fort and
every blessed war vessel in the place. May
the devil fly away with *El Rey Don Alfonso
XII.* for making his coronation so early!
From this moment I am a Carlist, heart and
soul! The shipping are all splendidly dressed
out and decorated with flags, and it is a beautiful sight. Unfortunately we have not suffi-
cient bunting to put the Josephine in gorgeous
array, so we remain in republican simplicity
with the old "Stars and Stripes" only at the
peak.

We went ashore to see the grand unfurling of the royal standard of Spain, which glorious event was to come off at nine o'clock in the *Parque de Isabella II.*, and thither we repaired. There was a great deal of dust and heat, and a mild display of *voluntarios* with a shaky band or two, crowds of people perspiring about the square, and lining the balconies and tops of the houses. In the middle of the square was a raised platform stand, like those used at political meetings in Union Square, but profusely adorned with yellow and red flags. About ten o'clock, after a grand flourish of trumpets, a number of carriages drove up, and set down a lot of splendid beings. They all ascended the tribune, with the Captain-General conspicuous in their midst; he taking from the hands of a trustworthy attendant the royal standard, and gracefully waving its heavy silken folds toward the crowd, shouted in a voice trembling with emotion (was it a bitter pill?): " *Ciududanos! El Etandarte Réal! Viva el Rey Alfonso Doce!* "

A moment of thrilling silence, and then three niggers in the crowd shouted: " *Viva el*

Rey!" after which they looked at each other
with a shame-faced kind of a grin, for not
another soul responded, and the great ceremony fell flatter than a buckwheat cake. I
only hope that poor Alfonso finds more encour-
agement at home.

We were very glad to get out of the sun and
dust and back to the schooner, to coolness and
breakfast, but even while resting from the
pleasant labors of that repast, the forts and
frigates all made it noon with twenty-one guns
apiece, close to us; and they did it all over
again at sundown. At night the city was
illuminated in all sorts of ways, but chiefly
with a highly smelly gas. I was out of sorts
and declined to go to the ball at the Casino,
which was to be a miraculously splendid concern. C—— and L——, went but soon came
back with the concise statement that the whole
thing was "beastly rot." To-morrow, however,
is to be the last sublimation of delirious joy
and loyalty; and as a final preparation, in the
silent watches of the night the statue (long
since deposed) of *Isabella Segunda* was restored
to its base in the *parque* which bears her

name. It was done almost surreptitiously, though by niggers who, I am afraid, were a little undignified in their proceedings. She was hoisted up by a rope round her marble neck, with a nigger *astride* on her—(let us say crupper), and there she remains "a joy of beauty and a thing forever."

January 24*th.*—The festivities to-day begin with a boat race in the harbor, and we are invaded by many citizens who come to participate in and witness the coming events. The agent of the Alexandre line, Mr. Todd, brought out a new and untried sail boat for the occasion, the " Adela," and he came off, too, to induce L—— to sail her for him in the race.

After a couple of very good gig races, the great match came off, with six sail boats entered, and we followed it about in the " City of Todd "—(the steam tender to the Alexandre line).

After a very clever and close eight mile race, the " Adela " won by a few feet, to the delirious joy of her owner; the race was only secured by L——'s skilful handling of the boat.

The moment this great event was decided we had to hasten ashore to witness the grand procession, representing all the provinces and possessions of Spain, which was to parade through the streets. Every balcony, doorway, and housetop, on the line of march, was crammed with people, mostly women in gorgeous array, and the house fronts decorated with palms and the broad leaves of the banana.

The procession was extraordinary—it was very pretty, and very funny. Porto Rico and Cuba were represented by Indians in a chariot loaded with growing tobacco and sugar cane. Castile, by ferocious Hidalgos in the costume of the period, and a total absence of the celebrated soap. And so they came on, an endless line of morrice dancers, sword players, knights, Don Pelayo, the Cid, Columbus, band of music, drummers, choral societies, each province accompanied by a chariot full of pretty and almost unattired young persons. Each province halted in the Plaza de Armas in front of the palace, and kicked up, played, danced, sang or whatever was the particular amusement of that province, and then passed on. It became so bewildering that we got tired of it long before the end—indeed, I think it lasted all night.

At the back of the *Casino* we discovered a theatre called the " *Cervantes*," which seemed attractive, so many were crowding in; so after paying for admission *to one act only*, we entered too, and found a good sized *salle* filled to over-flowing with nothing but men. One act of an awfully dull play was yawned through, and then the crowd was accounted for. An *entre acte* was given, just the most atrocious *can-can* I ever saw in my life, and the more dreadful things the performers did, the more vociferous were the yells and shrieks of delight from the pit. I thought of Molière : " *Un ballet ne sau-rait être trop long, pourvu que la morale soit bonne et la metaphysique bien entendue.*" In this aspect it was a very long ballet, and yet I don't usually moralize out of place.

January 25th.—Living on board a yacht is very much like living in the suburbs of a city. There is a *vis inertiœ* to overcome, especially in a hot climate, before the effort can be made to go ashore. I did go though, and found the town reposing in peace after the events of the last three days. I went over the Honradez cigarette factory, which is well worth seeing, especially the show workman who counts, rolls up and pastes a bundle, literally, while you are saying "Jack Robinson!" The usual daily supply required for the trade of the house is about two million cigarettes, and many of these are made by a very clever little machine, which being fed at the top with tobacco, and at the bottom with a lot of cut papers, fills the cigarette, rolls it tight, turn in the ends and throws it out into a basket; but a great many are made outside, and this explains why every porter or servant that one sees in the shops or dwelling, is always rolling cigarettes in his unemployed moments. It is the staple product next to cigars, and I suppose that there is no minute in the whole twenty-four hours, that some one is not either rolling, lighting, or smoking a cigarette.

January 26th.—We dined on board the

English corvette with a very pleasant party, and after dinner we were conducted on deck, and found a large assemblage to witness a minstrel performance by some of the crew. The theatrical arrangements were very good, the performance amusing; and how funny it was to hear from the sable actors, the good honest Lancashire dialect or the London cockney twang. The audience part of the crew were convulsed with laughter all the time, and were a capital part of the programme. It was a very pleasant finale to our stay here, for we hope to leave to-morrow.

January 27th.—We had to send one of our crew ashore to the hospital, with fever, and it is very difficult to replace him, so that we are detained one more day in port.

January 28th.—We passed the Morro Castle this morning with a fine breeze, close hauled and heading for the Gulf of Florida; we can almost lay our course, though the sea is heavy. How nice it is to be at sea again, and getting towards home too.

January 29*th.*—About dawn we sighted the light on the Double Headshot Keys, on Bahamas Banks, and stood on all day with a fair wind, but a "high norther" has been long expected, and the weather has given every warning of its approach. A nice time we shall have if it catches us in this narrow gulf. Vivid lightning in the N. W. this evening is looked upon as the immediate precursor of our expected visitor, and we make everything as snug as possible. One of the advantages of sea travel over locomotion on land, is the joy of anticipation.

January 30*th.*—We had a lively shaking up last night, but we have run far enough to the north, not only to escape the force of the norther, but to drop into a calm, and the sun shines out as bright as usual.

January 31*st.*—Last night heavy squalls ushered in a strong breeze from S.W., which soon ripened into a gale of wind, and made us shorten sail down to a reefed trysail, close reefed foresail, and bonnet off staysail. It has caught us in the Gulf stream, and in consequence has knocked up a most awful sea, which breaks all over us, and we are battened down unpleasantly in the cabin, without the slightest hope of keeping our feet. It rains too, violently and incessantly, and the sea seems getting worse every minute. I don't believe even Mark Tapley could have extracted any jolliness from the situation.

Towards evening the wind hauled to the northward, and the consoling opinion is that it will be worse before it is any better. We are hove-to, and there is nothing to do but to possess our souls with patience, hear the wind howling, and ride it out.

After three months of invariable sunshine and heat, it is an absolute phenomenon to witness a whole day of dark, ragged, rolling, oily-looking clouds, without a patch of blue sky, or any evidence that the sun ever existed, and to experience a cold that shivers the marrow of one's bones. And this, then, is what we used to long for in Trinidad!

C—— upset the salt cellar! Absit omen!

February **1st.** — The sun broke partly through the clouds this morning and his rays diffused a little comfort upon things, although it has been blowing hard **all** night and keeps on doing **so** and **more** also. The **N.W.** wind makes it very cold, and the China-blue sea **is** all confused and heaving about like extremely agile haystacks. We are still hove-to, and it looks as if a long future of hove-to were awaiting us.

At **4** P.M. the sea and the wind had both abated a little so that we could get some sail on her, and head **out** of the execrable Gulf stream, for which, **as** the mate truly puts it, **"** we've got no kind of use," and by dark we clear its well-defined boundaries to the westward, and find ourselves, almost by enchantment, free **from the** vile jumping and tumbling that made **life a** burden of holding **on, and** being bruised. **The sea is** comparatively **comfortable and grows** quieter every moment, so **we joyfully shake** out reefs, and although the **wind is ahead, this is a minor evil, and** enjoyment **and content once more become our guests.**

I must here record the admirable qualities and behavior **of the** "Josephine," under the quite trying conditions to which she was subjected. While we rolled gunwale under on each side, **we** dipped up comparatively little water, took very few seas over the bows, and only one of any importance into the cockpit; and after every roll, **pitch and** dive in the "scandalous" sea that was running and heaping **together from every quarter of the** compass, **she** would rise and give a buoyant little shake, like a fish-hawk after a dive for a mullet. **We** did **not** carry anything away, **or** part even the strand **of a** rope !

February 2d.—The **sun rose** brightly **and** warmly, with **a** light **fair** breeze and **smooth** sea, **but** in the afternoon a **heavy sea rolled in and** destroyed the **harmony of things a good deal.**

February 3d.—**Last night was a** beastly night. **The " all-fired " sea, as the** mate called **it, rolled us about and** shook **the rigging so** much, that **although a good breeze was blowing,** we tore the mainsail from the gaff, split the foresail and chafed a hole in the fore staysail. The rain is incessant, the sky lowering with ragged oily clouds, the sea brutal and everything is unlovely. We are scudding before a gale of wind, fortunately fair, under close reefs, through dirty green waves, as we are near the shore and about thirty miles from Charleston.

About noon we sighted the light-ship on Rattlesnake Shoals, and hauled our wind to beat up to the harbor, setting signal for a pilot, but it was blowing so hard that it looked as if we would have to remain at sea all night—not a cheerful prospect, with a rapidly falling barometer, and awfully cold weather. It is always the *revocare gradum* that is the labor and the sorrow, and the cold cuts like a sword on our sunburned and unaccustomed skins.

At last we see a little pilot-schooner bearing down to us, and were not sorry to see her boat launched, and the welcome that pilot received was supernaturally warm. We did not get up to the city till after dark though, as the weather set in very thick—but then—a quiet night!

February 4th.—IIow pleasant, to be snugly at anchor here, and listen to the horrid weather wreaking its vengeance outside.

> " A stiff nor wester's blowin', Bill ; oh, don't you hear
> it roar now.''

A dull, leaden, gloomy sky, and the thermometer at 42° are not pleasant accompaniments, and they admonish us to make everything as comfortable as possible for the ending to our cruise, which cannot fail to be as cold and disagreeable as the beginning of it has been delightful. So we put up a stove in the cabin, to the great joy of the two polly parrots, who, for the last day or two, have been shivering on their perches, and who at once begin uttering improper things in Spanish.

February 8th.—There is no need to describe Charleston. Almost everybody knows all about it.

L—— was stationed here in the blockading squadron during the war, and it is full of reminiscences for him. I am very glad to see it for the first time, although so evidently fallen from its high estate. The destruction of war is still traced in the many dilapidated buildings within the city, which has never recovered from its terrible effects. But whatever else it may have lost, the hospitality for which its citizens are renowned, still flourishes in full force ; we certainly were charmingly received, and dined and wined " promiscuous." I shall never forget a day's shooting that we had at John's Island, nor the depth of the river mud. Tired from a long day's tramp, I arrived at the water side to find the boat far below me, and between us was stretched a smooth, jellyish, treacherous plain of the most liquid and odoriferous slime, which had to be traversed. While shuddering on the brink, I was accosted by a nigger boy, who agreed for the consideration of "two bits" to carry me in safety on his back. In trepidation, mingled with a gentle hope, I mounted my sable steed, whose ivories showed from ear to ear as he took his first cautious step ; lower and lower he sank at each advance, till on reaching the deepest and blackest part, he slipped and over I went on my back ! What shrieks ! what yells of delight ! arose from the tug moored

safely out in the river! my own pickle I leave
entirely to the imagination, no words can describe it.

At length to-day our delightful visit comes
to an end, and with the morning tide and a
fair breeze we leave the jolly South Caro-
linians.

February 9th.—We had a very strong wester-
ly breeze last night, and we are now enjoying a
gale, cheerless, cold and revolting, with the
usual accompaniment of a heavy rough sea.

February 10th.—A beastly, stormy, tossy
night, so vile that as the wind is getting round
to the east with every prospect of a gale from
the N.E. we decide to run for Beaufort harbor for shelter; the cold was intense last night,
and the decks and rigging are covered with ice,
and the prospect of quiet anchorage under a
lee is full of charms.

We reached the entrance to the harbor about
2 o'clock, and setting signal for a pilot, stood
off and on, outside the foaming bar, but as no
pilot answered our signal, at dark we are

obliged to anchor for the night, but we are close in shore and the water is smooth.

February 11*th.*—Our anchorage outside the bar under the land as a shelter from the expected northeaster, very nearly proved our destruction. About midnight the weather changed, and the wind came on to blow a gale from the southeast, bringing us close on a lee shore and only a very little outside the breakers, with one of the crew sick and another totally useless. We got all sail on her as rapidly as possible in hopes of "clawing off," but it soon became evident that we could not heave in one link of her cable, and that if we slipped it we could never weather the fierce breakers on the bar. Meanwhile the whole sweep of the Atlantic was getting up a tremendous sea, and there was nothing left for us but to pay out sixty fathoms on the starboard anchor, which we did, also dropping the port anchor with forty-five fathoms, and then sat down to ride it out. All the remainder of the darkness, the fury and wrath of the gale increased, and the gallant little schooner was wildly plunging and tearing at her anchors while the rolling and tossing was tremendous.

When daylight broke, I never saw a wilder scene—the savage, frothing green seas came rolling past us, and breaking in thunder and foam just astern of us, sometimes very close alongside too, went tearing up on the beach, which, close as it was to us, was entirely concealed by the foam and misty spray—the screaming of the wind, and the wild roar of the waters were incessant and really awful, especially under the dead, leaden sky which I fancied I could almost touch—and we had to endure all this, because the pilot yesterday did not choose to respond to our signal !

About mid-day we had a bad scare; the wind, without abating, had begun to veer by the southward, and the breakers were so close to us that it was evident the anchors had dragged—*settled* the mate called it. This meant going ashore and a swim for it, besides leaving the bones of the little darling on this inhospitable shore. We found on examination that the cables had fouled, and this made things look quite grim. We got the trysail on her, which eased her somewhat, but in the midst of our anxiety a furious squall came up from the westward, accompanied by a tremendous fall of douches, a sort of giant rain, and this, veering the wind to the N.W., brought it right off shore to our great relief and joy. The barometer began to rise, so did our spirits, and though it blew as hard as ever, and we tumbled about fearfully, it was all right and we could turn in comfortably.

February 16*th*.—Though the swell is still considerable, the N.W. wind has knocked down the sea and the sun rises clear and fresh, while the cruel beach to which we were so perilously near yesterday, lies quietly basking like the crocodile in " Alice,"

> " Who welcomes little fishes in
> With gently smiling jaws,"

and the wavelets ripple on it as if they were the most innocent little frisking things, with no thought of evil. With some trouble we got in the anchors, and again hoist signals for the tardy pilot, who comes off in a row boat just as we are about to stand out to sea and desert the unfriendly place. A schooner with her sails all split to pieces passes in ahead of us, and about noon we drop anchor in smooth water.

The town of Beaufort is a miserable, shiftless looking place, with many signs of great poverty and some of unrequited labor: the shop-keepers lounge at the street corners, and rush into their stores at sight of an infrequent customer. The most comfortable looking and neatest cottages belong to colored people, and they seem to possess all the energy and most of the intelligence, although involuntary effects of the old slavery times still hang about them. I was much struck by the appearance of a district school, and the brightness as well as the neat cleanliness of the small colored scholars. On the other hand I was highly amused by a visit to the Court House, where a nigger was being tried for burglary accompanied with fracture of most of the Commandments. The judge, the jury, the counsel and all the spectators, were industriously using tobacco in its most unpleasant form, and I had no inclination to linger for the conclusion of the trial.

We underwent, ourselves, a most rigid examination from the Collector of the Port, but we were innocent of cigars or any form of smuggling.

February 13*th.*—Short-handed as we are, the remainder of the crew have made a protest against proceeding farther north, without ad- tional hands. In vain have we tried to procure any; not a man, colored or white, is willing to ship for the short trip round Hatteras. It is a great disappointment to L——, who was very anxious to return to the port we left, and com- plete the round cruise. But he yields to circum- stances, and has determined to lay the "Joseph- ine" up for the rest of the winter here, so that we shall proceed home by land.

It is a very serious moment, this ending of a cruise which has now lasted over three delight- ful months, and has been one of great enjoyment, infinite variety and unvaried good feeling. We part from the dear little schooner that has car- ried us so long and so well with deeper feelings, I think, than any of us care to show, soon to be scattered again in our different avocations of pleasure or business.

As we stand upon the shore, in the cold gray

of the morning, and turn to take one last look
at the poor little darling, sitting so gracefully
on the smooth dark water, it is like leaving
home. And I think of Dante's beauteous lines
with their almost passionate repetition, the tender expression of lingering, back-looking regret—

> " Senza più aspettar lasciái la riva
> Prendendo la campagna—lento lento ! "

Finis.

www.ingramcontent.com/pod-product-compliance
Lightning Source LLC
Chambersburg PA
CBHW020617030726
47497CB00007B/2281